Dear Dr. Rosenthal,
  It is a pleasure to be in touch with a fellow scholar interested in the same subject, and I hope that we can share our views in future emails or even face-to-face.

Red Apocalypse

The Religious Evolution of Soviet Communism

Arthur Jay Klinghoffer

University Press of America, Inc.
Lanham • New York • London

Copyright © 1996 by
University Press of America,® Inc.
4720 Boston Way
Lanham, Maryland 20706

3 Henrietta Street
London, WC2E 8LU England

All rights reserved
Printed in the United States of America
British Cataloging in Publication Information Available

Library of Congress Cataloging-in-Publication Data

Klinghoffer, Arthur Jay
Red apocalypse : the religious evolution of Soviet communism / Arthur Jay Klinghoffer.
p. cm.
Includes bibliographical references and index.
1. Communism and christianity. 2. Communism and christianity--Soviet Union. I. Title.
HX536.K555   1996   335.43--dc20   95-44783 CIP

ISBN 0-7618-0220-7 (cloth: alk: ppr.)
ISBN 0-7618-0221-5 (pbk: alk: ppr.)

⊖™ The paper used in this publication meets the minimum requirements of American National Standard for information Sciences—Permanence of Paper for Printed Library Materials, ANSI Z39.48—1984

To Libby Jones Klinghoffer,
who set my own evolution in motion —
thanks for your continued
encouragement of this research project.

Contents

I	Thy Kingdom Come	1

Historic Redemption

II	The Prophetic Jew	13
III	The End of Days	23
IV	The Religious Atheist	33
V	The Russified Mission	43
VI	Bolshevik on the Cross	57

The Communist Religion

VII	Tenets of Faith	67
VIII	The Spiritual Quest	79
IX	The Social Gospel	93

The Soviet Church

X	Laying the Foundations	109
XI	The Medieval Edifice	119
XII	From Renaissance to Counter-Reformation	129
XIII	The Soviet Enlightenment	141

Whither Communism?

XIV	Secularization and Religious Evolution	163
	Index	175

Chapter I

THY KINGDOM COME

It was 1991, and the Soviet Union was rapidly disintegrating. Monuments to Vladimir Ilyich Lenin, founder of the state, were being toppled throughout the country; statuary busts of the erstwhile communist hero were being ignominiously dragged through the streets. Calls were accelerating for the removal of Lenin's body from the mausoleum in Red Square, while Leningrad was reverting to its original name, St. Petersburg, following a public referendum. In one Russian town, a portrait of Lenin hanging in a first grade classroom was replaced with a poster of Mickey Mouse.[1] A crisis of communist religious faith gripped the collapsing Soviet Union. The Marxist-Leninist church's spiritual legitimacy was eroding, along with institutional edifices representing nearly three quarters of a century of the Bolshevik clergy's rule. Soon the Communist Party of the Soviet Union was illegal, the U.S.S.R. no longer existed as a unified state, and the discarded communist religion lay rumpled within the dustbin of history.

Despite avowed atheism, Soviet communism evolved as a secular religion bearing many institutional and doctrinal similarities to Christianity. "Red" baptisms and weddings were incorporated into the system, along with pseudo-Christian rites mimicking the holidays of Christmas and Easter. In fact, it should be realized that Christian values strongly influenced the precepts of Marxism-Leninism and that the course of Soviet communist development closely paralleled that of Christianity. Unconscious borrowing of values from the surrounding Christian society surely played a role, but so too did deliberate imitation. In some cases, similarity was not based on causality but was due to the fact that both communism and Christianity are mass institutionalized movements sharing many common characteristics.[2]

Recent assaults on the validity of Leninism should be viewed as a spiritual phenomenon as the Lenin cult included aspects of the sacred; the revered Vladimir Ilyich symbolically substituted for Jesus. He was treated as a messiah whose body was made immortal through embalming, and his tomb became a holy shrine. Demands for the removal of his corpse, and its possible burial, therefore struck at the very heart of communist religious doctrine. The disintegration of the Soviet communist system unleashed a virulent iconoclasm and Lenin, as the central focus of devotion, was rapidly desanctified.

Religion in Red

Communism denies the existence of God and is devoid of supernatural attributes often associated with religion. Nevertheless, it provides a framework for contemplating good and evil, the relationship between man and the universe, and the ultimate in man's existence. It views history as driven by a force external to man and depicts man as fulfilling a grand mission in quest of a determined goal. Communism, as has been recognized by many prominent theologians, historians and social scientists, therefore exhibits qualities which classify it as a religion. Protestant theologian Reinhold Niebuhr, Harvard historian Crane Brinton, British economist John Maynard Keynes and French political sociologist Raymond Aron must be included in this group as well as William Bullitt, first American ambassador to the Soviet Union, and Archbishop Fulton Sheen, noted Catholic clergyman of the airwaves.[3] Others have similarly described Soviet communism as "secular religion," "theocracy," "atheist theocracy," "secular theocracy," or "secular Christianity."[4]

Perhaps atheistic communism does not qualify as a bona fide religion, but it nevertheless functions as one and may be analyzed in religious terms.[5] Even intellectuals who refuse to accept communism as a religion often admit that it serves as a substitute for religion.[6] This aspect of Soviet communism was particularly alarming to anti-communist Christians who saw the suppression of their own religion in the U.S.S.R. as part of a competition for men's souls and ultimate commitment. To them, the communist "quasi-religion" had usurped the spiritual authority of the true religion, Christianity.[7]

French man of letters Andre Gide is said to have declared that "he had always been a Communist at heart, without knowing it, even when he had been most Christian."[8] Such an insight helps clarify the religious fusion that has often taken place between communism and Christianity, particularly in the Soviet Union. Polish Nobel laureate in literature Czeslaw Milosz has pointed out that many Christians in the U.S.S.R. saw Stalin acting in accordance with the will of God. In fact, many schools in Ukraine and Byelorussia displayed a crucifix between portraits of Lenin and Stalin and Soviet homes frequently included Lenin's countenance among icons hanging on the wall.[9] As will be demonstrated, such a symbiotic relationship is not quite fortuitous as Soviet communism borrowed from Christianity and, at times, intentionally modeled itself along Christian lines in an effort to attract believers to a new faith.

Toward Salvation

Communism and Christianity have similar origins, leading to the observation that conflict between them is "fratricidal."[10] Both derive from Jewish messianism, with Marx's Old Testament prophetism being overtaken by bureaucratic Leninism and Jesus' by the institutionalized Church. In essence, Leninism came to dominate Marxism-Leninism and Christianity evolved away from Judaic roots.

Communism and Christianity grew out of social protest directed at corrupt authority, and their responses stressed a communalism in which the private interest was subservient to the collective good. Marx's crusade failed to galvanize the proletarian masses of Western Europe, just as Jesus' mission did not attract widespread support among the Jews of Roman Palestine. Persecution accompanied a belief in the imminence of deliverance, and both men died without seeing their dreams reach earthly fruition. Neither is buried at the place of ostensible triumph. Marx lies beneath Highgate Cemetery in London, far removed from Red Square, while Jesus is presumably entombed in Jerusalem rather than at St. Peter's in Rome. Contrary to the hopes of both, their causes were adopted as the tools of empire, Soviet and Roman, and their doctrines spread by political fiat rather than individual conversions of conscience.[11]

Communism and Christianity present similar interpretations of the fall and redemption, compatible images of a secular utopia or heaven, and common themes of the struggle between good and evil, proletariat vs. bourgeoisie or Christ vs. the Anti-Christ. Transition is seen toward an earthly or otherwordly Kingdom of God, known either through historical materialist interpretation or revelation, and man prepares for his passage through internal spiritual transformation as a "New Soviet

Man" or born-again Christian filled with grace. Both religions have effectively sustained themselves, even though the goals of pure communism and the Kingdom of God have not been attained. In the communist case, the means have substituted for the ends and contradicted them as a dictatorship of the proletariat replaced the anticipated withering away of the state. In Christianity, the focus has been shifted from the Kingdom of God to salvation through faith in the Church. Eventually, central coordination of worldwide movements was undermined by nationalistic challenges which generated divergent sources of authority and faith; institutional control over society was also confronted by secularization, which removed various spheres of life from the religious domain.

Patterns

Communism not only reflects numerous aspects of Christianity, but its religious evolution is strikingly parallel.[12] Without exaggerating via any neo-determinist analysis, instructive analogies may be drawn. Karl Marx, for example, may be interpreted as an Old Testament prophet, a social critic railing against injustice and presenting the proletariat as his new chosen people. Marx viewed history as purposeful and linear, as a progression toward a secular Kingdom of God. His religious vision provided a bridge between Old and New Testament thinking, a la John the Baptist, and his Jewish prophetism was linked to a societal analysis echoing aspects of the Book of Revelation.

Lenin Russified Marxism and developed the Bolshevik religion out of his country's influential nineteenth century Christian socialist mode of thought; themes of suffering, the Third Rome (as the spiritual heir to Rome and Constantinople) and the sacredness of the Kremlin were thus incorporated into the Soviet system. Lenin had a close relationship with dissident Orthodox movements known as the Sectarians, and there was also an important group within the Bolshevik Party called the "Godbuilders" which wanted to substitute Bolshevism for Christianity by developing a religion centered on man. In an historic sense, Lenin may be compared to both Jesus and Paul, as a messiah who constructed the edifice of his own religion. Stalinism may then be related to the Crusades and Inquisition, with the demonization of Trotsky a reminder of the anti-Semitic strands evident within medieval Catholicism.

With Khrushchev came the Renaissance, exhibited in the cultural "Thaw" and de-Stalinization, and the Reformation, exemplified by the growth of national communisms within the bloc and experimentation with capitalist economic techniques. Brezhnev's Counter-Reformation, featuring a partial rapprochement with the Stalinist past, was then followed by Gorbachev's Enlightenment which stressed humanism, individualism and the separation of the communist church from the state. The Soviet system became secularized and, in common with developments in the European Enlightenment, faced a crisis of faith and a rise in nationalist fervor among both Russians and members of minority nationalities. It soon imploded, leaving communist institutions in shambles.

Synthesis

There has been a noticeable increase in intellectual intercourse between communists and Christians, fostering a greater recognition of shared concepts and concerns. Advocates of enhanced mutual understanding argue that man must supersede hierarchical church authority and freedom must be attained through the termination of exploitation or, in the Christian sense, by saving the soul.[13] Commitment to one's religious cause is affirmed, but organized churches are seen as corrupted. Soviet poet Yevgeny Yevtushenko attested to his faith in communism as an ideal and, in comparative reference to Christianity, proclaimed: "Neither can I, a believing communist, equate the substance of my religion with the crooks who climb on its band-wagon, with its inquisitors, its crafty, avaricious priests or its double-thinking, double-faced parishioners."[14] Christian theologian Jurgen Moltmann, a participant in the so-called "Marxist-Christian dialogue," has similarly identified with what he sees as the more pure revolutionary wing of his religion rather than with its state-linked institutional wing, a contrast which through analogy he relates to Marxist humanism in preference to Stalinism.[15]

Marxism may be viewed as the message of the Gospels adapted to the industrial age, particularly in reference to the adage of the last one now later being first.[16] So too with Paul's dictum in his Second Letter to the Thessalonians (3:10) that he who does not work, neither shall he eat. This saying reappeared in article twelve of the 1936 Soviet constitution, which stayed in effect for forty-one years. Indeed, some Christians see Marxism as an atheistic continuation of Jesus' mission and as a reflection of Christianity's failure to alleviate social conditions. According to this interpretation Christian neglect of the exploited engendered communism's ascent, but growing acceptance of justice through change is now pervading Christianity.[17] Marxist concern with false gods and idols, incorporated into the concept of alienation, is also penetrating Christian theology and, paradoxically, approval of violence as a legitimate instrument of change is growing within Christianity at a time when it is being jettisoned as a tenet of communist faith.[18]

The Catholic Church has traditionally viewed communism with hostility and has repeatedly made it anathema since Pope Pius IX's 1846 denunciation. Pius XI's 1937 "Divini Redemptoris" was especially harsh, but considerable moderation was later evident in Pope John XXIII's 1963 "Pacem in Terris." John XXIII also had an historic meeting in March 1963 with Aleksei Adzhubei, Khrushchev's son-in-law and editor of *Izvestiya*, and Paul VI received Soviet president Nikolai Podgorny in January 1967.[19] Mikhail Gorbachev conferred with Pope John Paul II on two occasions, in December 1989 and November 1990.

Although the Vatican is still doctrinally opposed to communism, it no longer eschews an exchange of ideas. However, Catholic liberation theologians have gone far beyond the Church of Rome in developing a fusion of Marxist and Christian concepts. They maintain that Christianity may coopt Marxist values, just as it incorporated Aristotelianism, and that its prime responsibility must be social justice. Pastoral activity is more essential than doctrine as the emphasis must be on group oriented action, or praxis. Jose Miranda, a Mexican Christian communist, has so closely fused communism and Christianity that he depicts Jesus as a communist.[20]

Liberation theologians accentuate the earthly aspects of their calling, looking forward (in common with Jews) to salvation within history through a process of humanization.[21] Little concern is shown toward saving souls in the afterlife as the Kingdom of God is seen as palpable and imminent. In fact, these theologians claim that this was the view of Jesus himself. Man must achieve it in this life, and the Church should "proclaim its own provisory character" (a concept analogous to the communist "withering away of the state") in preparation for its advent.[22]

Some Christians have lamented that the "Marxist-Christian dialogue" has been a one-way street, with little Christianity being woven into the Marxist fabric.[23] This was basically an accurate assessment, but the situation has changed considerably due to major adjustments in the Soviet Union and Eastern Europe during the late eighties. Communist-ruled systems became more tolerant of Christianity and, as will be demonstrated, they started to infuse Christianity into their political and sociological perspective. Leon Onikov, a career activist and ideologist within the Communist Party of the Soviet Union, declared shortly before its political demise: "The ideas of socialism were first formulated by Jesus Christ in the New Testament."[24]

Notes

1 National Public Radio, September 24, 1991. In Prague, Czechoslovakia, the journal of the world communist movement has ceased publication and its editorial headquarters have been returned to Catholic theologians for use as a seminary. Ironically, the building had continued to sport statues of Moses and Jesus in its facade during the lengthy communist interregnum. For information on the demise of *Problems of Peace and Socialism*, see Sergei Belenkov, "The Journal Gone, Problems Remain," *New Times*, no. 25 (June 19-25, 1990):ll.

2 The author is indebted to Stuart Charme for his keen methodological observations.

3 Charles West, *Communism and the Theologians* (New York: Macmillan, 1958), p. 132; Crane Brinton, *Ideas and Men: The Story of Western Thought* (Englewood Cliffs: Prentice-Hall, 1963), p. 374; John Maynard Keynes, excerpts from *A Short View of Russia*, *New Times*, no. 34 (August 21-27, 1990):40-41; Raymond Aron, *The Opium of the Intellectuals* (New York: W.W. Norton, 1957), p. 318; Beatrice Farnsworth, *William C. Bullitt and the Soviet Union* (Bloomington: Indiana University Press, 1967), p. 151 and Fulton Sheen, *Communism and the Conscience of the West* (Indianapolis: Bobbs-Merrill, 1948), p. 190. For other depictions of Soviet communism as a religion, see Will Herberg, *Faith Enacted as History* (Philadelphia: Westminster Press, 1976), p. 180; Jules Monnerot, *Sociology and Psychology of Communism* (Boston: Beacon Press, 1960), pp. 144-45 and 158; Jacques Ellul, *The New Demons* (New York: Seabury Press, 1975), p. 170; Harold Fallding, *The Sociology of Religion* (Toronto: McGraw-Hill Ryerson, 1974), pp. 28, 167 and 232; Lester DeKoster, *Communism and Christian Faith* (Grand Rapids: William Eerdmans, 1956), p. l; Rene Fueloep-Miller, *The Mind and Face of Bolshevism* (New York: Harper and Row, 1965), p. 72; Christel Lane, *The Rites of Rulers* (Cambridge: Cambridge University Press, 1981), p. 41; Matthew Spinka, *Christianity Confronts Communism* (New York: Harper and Brothers, 1936), p. 162 and Glenn Vernon, *Sociology of Religion* (New York: McGraw-Hill, 1962), pp. 80-81.

4 Nathan Leites, *The Operational Code of the Politburo* (New York: McGraw-Hill, 1951), p. xiv; Eduard Heimann, *Reason and Faith in Modern Society* (Middletown, Connecticut: Wesleyan University Press, 1961), p. 153; Robert V. Daniels, *The Nature of Communism* (New York: Random House, 1962), p. 328; Eduard Heimann, "Atheist Theocracy," *Social Research*, vol. 20, no. 3 (Fall, 1973):311; John Dziak, "The Study of the Soviet Intelligence and Security System," in Roy Godson, ed., *Comparing Foreign Intelligence* (Washington, D.C.: Pergamon-Brassey's, 1988), p. 67 and Paul Oestreicher in Paul Oestreicher, ed., *The Christian-Marxist Dialogue* (Toronto: Macmillan, 1969), p. 4.

5 See Nicholas Vakar, *The Taproot of Soviet Society* (New York: Harper and Brothers, 1961), p. 118 and Alfred Meyer, *Leninism* (New York: Praeger, 1957), p. 286. Aleksandr Yakovlev, a member of the Soviet Politburo and a close adviser to Mikhail Gorbachev, has written: "As a result of religion, atheism has its church followers, its prophets, its icons, its tombs, its relics, its holy writings, its heresies and dogmas, its orthodoxy, its catechism, its system of persecuting heretics, its repentance and renunciation. And, of course its Inquisition, which Stalin perfected with extreme fanatical cruelty." See *The Fate of Marxism in Russia* (New Haven and London: Yale University Press, 1993), p. 43.

6 Milovan Djilas, *The Unperfect Society: Beyond the New Class* (New York: Harcourt, Brace and World, 1969), pp. 38 and 40; William Hordern, *Christianity, Communism and History* (London: Lutterworth Press, 1957), p. 163; John Bennett, *Christianity and Communism Today* (New York: Association Press, 1966), pp. 45-46 and Carlton J.H. Hayes, *Nationalism: A Religion* (New York: Macmillan, 1960), p. 15.

7 See Merrimon Cuninggim, "The Undiscussable Topic," in Merrimon Cuninggim, ed., *Christianity and Communism* (Dallas: Southern Methodist University Press, 1958), pp. 12-13.

8 As cited by Enid Starkie in Richard Crossman, ed., *The God That Failed* (New York: Bantam, 1954), p. 166.

9 Czeslaw Milosz, *The Captive Mind* (New York: Vintage Books, 1951), p. 99; Vakar, p. 125 and Sherwood Eddy, *The Challenge of Russia* (New York: Farrar and Rinehart, 1931), p. 181.

10 Oestreicher, p. 4.

11 See Hordern, p. 70 and Christopher Dawson, *The Movement of World Revolution* (New York: Sheed and Ward, 1959), p. 79.

12 For similarities between the evolutions of Marxism and religions, see S.F. Kissin, *Farewell to Revolution* (New York: St. Martin's, 1978), pp. 50 and 65.

13 See Yuri Furmanov, "Renewing Christ and Marx," *New Times*, no. 22 (May 29-June 4, 1990):30-31.

14 Yevgeny Yevtushenko, *A Precocious Autobiography* (London: Collins and Harvill, 1963), p. 40.

15 Jurgen Moltmann in Thomas Ogletree, ed., *Openings for Marxist-Christian Dialogue* (New York: Abingdon Prerss, 1968), p. 56

16 See Louis Halle, "Marx's Religious Drama," *Encounter*, vol. XXV, no. 4 (October, 1965):37.

17 Robert Adolfs, "Church and Communism," in Oestreicher, pp. 35 and 127; Bennett, p. 19 and Oestreicher, p. 5.

18 See Ogletree, pp. 45-46 and Arthur McGovern, *Marxism: An American Christian Perspective* (Maryknoll. N.Y.: Orbis, 1980), p. 286.

19 See Adolfs, p. 29 and Peter Nichols, *The Politics of the Vatican* (New York: Praeger, 1968), p. 207.
20 Roger Haight, *An Alternative Vision: An Interpretation of Liberation Theology* (Mahwah, N.Y.: Paulist Press, 1985), pp. 20 and 263-64; Leonardo Boff, *Church: Charism and Power* (New York: Crossroad, 1985), p. 107 and Jose Miranda, *Communism in the Bible* (Maryknoll, N.Y.: Orbis, 1982), pp. 7-8.
21 Haight, p. 42.
22 Boff, p. 64.
23 Peter Hebblethwaite, *The Christian-Marxist Dialogue* (New York: Paulist Press, 1977), p. 112 and Dale Vree, *On Synthesizing Marxism and Christianity* (New York: John Wiley, 1976), p. 6.
24 Leon Onikov, "A Renewed Party Needs New Rules," *New Times*, no. 22 (May 29-June 4, 1990):35.

HISTORIC REDEMPTION

Chapter II

THE PROPHETIC JEW

Karl Marx, atheistic and in some ways anti-Semitic, was nevertheless a prophet in the Old Testament tradition. Descended from rabbis on both sides of his family, he was born in 1818 into a religiously transitional household. His father, a bureaucrat in the German court system, had converted to Protestantism in 1816 as a means of social mobility and Karl was baptized at age six. His mother delayed her conversion to 1825 pending the death of her rabbinic father. Karl received an extensive Biblical education in secondary school, learning much about Judaism through a Christian prism. His doctoral dissertation dealt with religious themes and he absorbed theological insights from his study of Hegel, Saint-Simon and Feuerbach. Marx had to struggle with his Jewish origins in a predominantly Christian milieu, and he had to endure a life of penury and exile in England. Combined with his critical vision of capitalist exploitation, Marx's personal experiences contributed to the molding of a radical consumed with life's injustices, of a revolutionary exhorting the restructuring of society, of a Hebrew prophet preparing man for the industrial age.

Torah Redux

Old Testament prophets were often alienated from their societies and unconcerned about their personal status; self-imposed exile was frequently the result.[1] Jewish theologian Abraham Heschel has revealingly written: "The prophet is an iconoclast, challenging the apparently holy, revered, and awesome. Beliefs cherished as certainties, institutions endowed with supreme sanctity, he exposes as scandalous pretensions."[2] Prophets do not sugarcoat reality and, in a passage reminiscent of Marx's critique of capitalism, philosophy professor Howard Parsons has declared: "The prophet calls men back to their true selves, disowns their false selves, warns them of the harvest of unhappiness in living by the false self, and promises them the rewards of living by the true self."[3]

Old Testament prophets demanded social justice through political action as they emotionally attempted to shock the populace into accepting the need for change. History was viewed as a redemptive mission as direction and purpose were discerned, and a day of reckoning was threatened if man did not alter his ways.[4] The rightness in reality spoke through the prophet, and history represented hope.[5] The role of the prophet, according to Heschel, was "to disclose the future in order to illume what is involved in the present." God was the underlying force, and history was "the vessel for His action" just as the word was "the vessel for His revelation."[6]

Prophets, as Jewish realists, concentrated on this world and paid scant attention to an afterlife or immortality. Humankind on earth was the prime concern, and their reflections on God began and ended with man. Critical but optimistic, they stressed what man might be rather than what he was.[7]

Marxism has been recognized by numerous scholars as a secularized version of Hebrew prophesy, with theologian Karl Lowith asserting that *The Communist Manifesto* is pervaded with a "religious spirit of prophetism,"and Israeli historian J.L. Talmon maintaining that Marx was in the "prophetic and Talmudic tradition."[8] Even the Soviet Union's first commissar responsible for education and culture, Anatoly Lunacharsky, recognized Jewish and prophetic roots in Marxism; he saw Marx as part of a continuum extending from Isaiah through Jesus, Paul and Spinoza.[9] Historian Christopher Dawson avers that Marx "was one of those exiles of Israel like Spinoza, whose isolation from the religious community of their fathers only serves to intensify their proud consciousness of a prophetic mission."[10] Indeed, Marx was in the tradition of "free prophets" such as Amos, Hosea, Micah, Jeremiah and Ezekiel who were not paid by either the court or the temple and who claimed that they understood the will of God better than did the kings and priests.[11]

Marx's vision may be related to Hebraic themes such as the egalitarianism practiced in pre-monarchic Israel or God entering into a covenant with a people pursuing justice, basing it on collective responsibility.[12] The fundamental message is the deliverance of the oppressed and, in a Jewish rather than Christian vein, it is the poor rather than the weak who shall inherit the earth.[13] The proletariat serves, mutatis mutandis, as the chosen people,[14] although it could be argued that the victorious proletariat was at first expected to institute class rule rather than dispense justice (Protestant theologian Paul Tillich points out that the proletariat is to fulfill an historic mission, rather than embody a moral quality).[15] Marx, however, clearly had a religious and ethical fervor when commenting on the proletarian cause. His emotional commitment superseded his rationalism as Marx expounded upon the proletariat's calling before he actually analyzed working class behavior through his methodology of historical materialism. The issue of proletarian organization during the revolution was almost totally neglected.

Intellectual parallels between Marxism and Biblical Judaism are evident without resort to ad hominem references to Karl Marx's Jewish background. Nevertheless, this latter factor may have played a role in the formulation of Marx's societal perspective. Russian philosopher Nicolas Berdyaev believed that subconscious Judaism influenced Marx's views on the revolt of the proletariat, and theologian Joseph Petulla linked the proletariat's liberating role to Marx's recognition of the oppression experienced by European Jewry.[16] British philosopher Isaiah Berlin presented a differing interpretation in which Marx was portrayed as an anti-Semitic Jew who stressed the proletarian mission as a means of escaping from his own heredity; both religion and nationalism were consequently underestimated.[17]

The Guiding Hand

Marxism, although based on perceived scientific laws rather than God's revelation, echoes Old Testament concepts ("the end of days") regarding salvation through a linear historical process. Judaism, in contrast to a religion such as Buddhism which adheres to a cyclical interpretation, delineates an underlying purpose in history ("As I have planned, so shall it be, and as I have purposed, so shall it stand." - Isaiah, 14:24) as it progresses toward a goal. Man finds fulfillment within history as there is movement in the direction of an eschaton, an ultimate point at which justice will be served.[18] Judaism and Marxism are eschatological and share the non-dualistic view that redemption, which for the Marxist takes place through a socialist revolution and the establishment of a classless society, is earthly and within history. They are also teleological as there is a final cause bearing essential goodness that provides life with meaning, and human activity is considered purposive rather than functional. History embodies its own meaning and is not merely a preparatory stage for another existence. Man's future on earth may be qualitatively different, with unethical or unpleasant aspects of reality being negated.[19] Idolatry and false values are to be eliminated ("Again the word of the Lord came unto me, saying Son of man, cause Jerusalem to know her abominations." - Ezekiel, 16:1-2) and it is therefore not surprising that Marx devoted most of his attention to exposing the perversity of capitalism and wrote little about his envisioned classless society.

Marx's eschatological vision so dominated his analytic perspective that it took precedence over his better scientific judgment. According to Marx's methodology of historical materialism, no stage of history may ever become permanent since some contradictory force, unleashed by the dialectic, must challenge the existing order and produce a new synthesis through structural change. Nevertheless, Marx believed that communism would be the final historic stage, producing no antithesis as exploitation would have been ended and classes eliminated. Surely Marx was at variance with his own dialectic. For him, communism was not just the objective result of man's evolution as viewed by a social scientist but a desirable goal imbued with positive qualitative content. Marx did not just expect communism, he longed for it and worked toward its realization. No antithesis could be contemplated once society was, in Marx's view, without defect. Like the Jews, Marx discerned a basic goodness in man so perfectibility could be anticipated. [20]

Czechoslovak philosopher Milan Machovec maintains with keen insight that Marx's endorsement of historical materialism, but rejection of fate, is similar to the Jewish affirmation of God but denial of predestination.[21] Fatalism means inevitability without human action, while Marx clearly believed that man's autonomy was essential. It may be true that "the 'God' of communism . . . is a God of inevitability," but man controls the pace.[22] Although he may be conditioned by economic forces, they can only create his consciousness; he must then act. In any case, the structures which condition man are built and transformed by him. While the course of history is inevitable, it is not automatic and this belief strongly influences those Marxists who stress praxis, or man as activist.[23] Jews and Christian liberation theologians share this perspective.

There has always been a tension (evident in most religions) between the determinist aspects of Marx's eschatology and the concept of free will, although scholars are in basic agreement that the late Marx was more determinist and the early Marx more voluntarist. Utopianism is often associated with the voluntarist explanation as Utopians depend upon human action due to incertitude that their goals will be achieved.[24] Academic controversy over Marx's determinism or free will is hardly illuminating, the issue being more semantic than substantive. Once determinism is dissociated from connotations of fatalism, a degree of free will is recognized. Intellectual historian Crane Brinton has written: "Once more, we can only note that mataphysical belief in determinism seems for the Marxist, as for the Calvinist, quite consonant with a psychological belief in the importance of the will to believe - and act - in the individual."[25]

Karl Marx, the communist atheist, incorporated Jewish themes and values into his treatment of history. Marxism was therefore pervaded with religiosity; as we shall see, it additionally provided a framework out of which was to come a new messiah.

Notes

1. Howard Parsons, "The Prophetic Mission of Karl Marx," in Herbert Aptheker, ed., *Marxism and Christianity* (New York: Humanities Press, 1968), p. 145. Psycho-historian Bruce Mazlish maintains that revolutionary ascetics exhibit displaced libidos as human considerations are subordinated to devotion to the cause. See *The Revolutionary Ascetic:Evolution of a Political Type* (New York: McGraw-Hill, 1976), pp. 5-6.
2. Abraham Heschel, *The Prophets* (Philadelphia: Jewish Publication Society of America, 1962), p. 10. See also John Lewis, "Communism the Heir to the Christian Tradition," in John Lewis, Karl Polanyi and Donald Kitchin, eds., *Christianity and the Social Revolution* (New York: Charles Scribner's Sons, 1936), pp. 473-74.
3. Parsons, p. 153.
4. See Erich Fromm, *You Shall Be As Gods* (New York: Holt, Rinehart and Winston, 1966), p. 118 and Parsons, p. 153.
5. Parsons, p. 147 and Jan Milic Lochman, *Encountering Marx* (Philadelphia: Fortress Press, 1977), p. 118.
6. Heschel, pp. 12 and 168-69.
7. See John Macmurray, *Creative Society* (New York: Association Press, 1936), p. 56 and Parsons, p. 160.
8. Harold Fallding, *The Sociology of Religion* (Toronto: McGraw-Hill Ryerson, 1974), p. 37; Milovan Djilas, *The Unperfect Society: Beyond the New Class* (New York: Harcourt, Brace and World, 1969), p. 42; Martin Seliger, *The Marxist Conception of Ideology* (Cambridge: Cambridge University Press, 1977), p. 184; Isaiah Berlin, *Against the Current* (New York: Viking, 1980), pp. 282-83; Jacques Ellul, *The New Demons* (New York: Seabury Press, 1975), p. 167; Raymond Aron, *The Opium of the Intellectuals* (New York: W.W. Norton, 1957), p. 267; Herndon Wagers, "Is Communism a Christian Heresy?," in Merrimon Cuninggim, ed., *Christianity and Communism* (Dallas: Southern Methodist University Press, 1958), p. 79; Reinhold Niebuhr, "Christian Politics and Communist Religion," in Lewis, Polanyi and Kitchin, p. 462; Trevor Ling, *Buddha, Marx, and God* (New York: St. Martin's, 1966), p. 140; M.B. Foster, "Historical Materialism," in D.M. Mackinnon, *Christian Faith and Communist Faith* (London: Macmillan, 1953), p. 93; Karl Lowith, *Meaning in History* (Chicago: University of Chicago Press, 1949), p. 44 and J.L. Talmon, "The Jewish Intellectuals in Politics, *Midstream*, vol. XII, no. 1 (January 1966):7. Jewish theologian Martin Buber dissents from this interpretation, arguing that prophetism emphasizes human participation while Marxism is based on a more ordained apocalyptic eschatology. See *Paths in Utopia* (Boston: Beacon Press,), p. 10. See also Kenelm Burridge, *New Heaven, New Earth* (New York: Schocken, 1969), p. 131.

9 George Kline, *Religious and Anti-Religious Thought in Russia* (Chicago: University of Chicago Press, 1968), p. 118.
10 Christopher Dawson, *The Dynamics of World History* (New York: New American Library, 1962), p. 348.
11 David Aune distinguishes between four types of Israelite prophets: shamanistic, cult and temple, court and free. See *Prophesy in Early Christianity and the Ancient Mediterranean World* (Grand Rapids: William Eerdmans, 1983), pp. 83-85.
12 Joseph Petulla, *Christian Political Theology: A Marxian Guide* (Maryknoll, N.Y.: Orbis, 1972), pp. 230-31 and James Adams, Is Marx's Thought Relevant to the Christian?: A Protestant View," in Nicholas Lobkowicz, ed., *Marx and the Western World* (Notre Dame: University of Notre Dame Press, 1967), p. 380.
13 Reinhold Niebuhr, *Moral Man and Immoral Society* (New York: Charles Scribner's Sons, 1932), p. 154.
14 Lowith, p. 37 and Nicolas Berdyaev, *The Russian Revolution* (Ann Arbor: University of Michigan Press, 1966), p. 38.
15 Paul Tillich, *The Protestant Era* (Chicago: University of Chicago Press, 1948), pp. 25-26.
16 Berdyaev, pp. 69-70 and Petulla, p. 88.
17 Berlin claims that, for psychological reasons, Marx identified with the concept of a powerful proletariat as a mechanism to compensate for what he perceived as Jewish weakness. Marx's Jewishness was suppressed, and his anger against his people and his middle class father surfaced in his negative portrayal of the bourgeoisie, whom he identified with the Jews. See *Against the Current* (New York: Viking, 1980), pp. 277-86.
18 Foster, p. 93; Adams, p. 379; Wagers, p. 80 and Jose Miranda, *Marx and the Bible* (Maryknoll, N.Y.: Orbis, 1974), p. 87.
19 Crane Brinton, *Ideas and Men: The Story of Western Thought*, second edition (Englewood Cliffs: Prentice Hall, 1963), p. 377; Erich Fromm, *Psychoanalysis and Religion* (New Haven: Yale University Press, 1950), pp. 117-18; Tillich, pp. 253-54; Thomas Ogletree in Thomas Ogletree, ed., *Openings for Marxist-Christian Dialogue* (New York: Abingdon Press, 1968), p. 27 and Reinhold Niebuhr, *The Nature and Destiny of Man*, vol. 2 (New York: Charles Scribner's Sons, 1964), p. 287. For an argument that Marxism is not eschatological, see Norman Levine, "Humanism Without Eschatology," *Journal of the History of Ideas*, vol. 33, no. 2 (April-June, 1972):298.
20 Marx's subordination of all concerns to the just proletarian cause produced an absolutist interpretation whose ethics could be viewed in terms of the ends superseding the means. See Niebuhr, "Christian Politics and Communist Religion," p. 465.
21 Milan Machovec, *A Marxist Looks at Jesus* (Philadelphia: Fortress Press, 1976), p. 58.

22 William Hordern, *Christianity, Communism and History* (London: Lutterworth Press, 1957), p. 82.
23 Jacques Maritain, *True Humanism*, sixth edition (London: Geoffrey Bles, 1954), p. 123; John B.S. Haldane, *The Marxist Philosophy and the Sciences* (Freeport, N.Y.: Books for Libraries Press, 1969), p. 37; Roger Garaudy, *The Alternative Future* (New York: Simon and Schuster, 1974), p. 182 and Reinhold Niebuhr, "The Religion of Communism," *Atlantic Monthly*, vol. CXLVII (April, 1931):463.
24 See Lewis Coser, "Millenarians, Totalitarians and Utopians," *Dissent*, vol. 5 no. 1 (Winter, 1958):72 and Buber, p. 8.
25 Brinton, p. 378.

Chapter III

THE END OF DAYS

Marxism includes underlying themes of messianism and apocalypticism derived from Judaism but later accentuated by Christianity. It also presents a schema reminiscent of Daniel's Old Testament delineation of a Kingdom of God, although its millenarian interpretation has strong Christian overtones generally associated with the Book of Revelation. While the Jewish component of Marx's writings is evident, it is not necessarily representative of the mainstream of ancient Israelite thought but rather of those aspects of Judaism that were afforded a prominent place within Christian theology.

Forces of Light

Karl Marx's view of the proletariat liberating the economically exploited, and ushering in a classless society with no private propety or money, is messianic and complementary to his basic eschatology.[1] This messianism harkens back to the ancient Jewish tradition and is linked to the later Talmudic idea that the messiah was "born" when the Second Temple was destroyed. His coming would then lead to the reunification of Jews dispersed in the diaspora. Marx's Jewish heritage probably had some influence on his societal analysis ("For I know your manifold transgressions and your mighty sins: they afflict the just, they take a bribe, and they turn aside the poor in the gate from their right." - Amos, 5:12) but it would be difficult to verify Christopher Dawson's claim that Marx had repressed religious instincts as he could not adapt to the Gentile world as did his father. His messianism, according to this account, then represented the alienation of the Jews from Christian society or, symbolically, the antagonism of the proletariat toward the bourgeoisie.[2]

Messianism developed among the Jews in the eighth century B.C. as a reaction to the Assyrian subjugation of the kingdoms of Judah and Israel. As portrayed by Isaiah, Micah and Zechariah the messiah was to be an earthly political leader, a successor in the line of David who would restore Jewish glory. Later, during the Babylonian exile of the sixth century B.C., a different conception of the messiah was formulated by prophets such as Ezekiel and the Second Isaiah. Perhaps influenced by Zoroastrianism, the emphasis was on an otherwordly, spiritual and transcendent figure.[3] This latter interpretation was then advanced during the early second century B.C. by Daniel and Enoch during a period of Jewish rebellion against the Greco-Syrian ruler Antiochus Epiphanes. The Book of Daniel was written approximately 167-164 B.C.; the Book of Enoch, possibly assembled by several authors over a century, traces its origins back to 170 B.C. while the killing of the revolutionary Judah Maccabee, the hero of Hannukah, took place in 160 B.C.. Daniel and Enoch discussed a heavenly "Son of Man," and Daniel also commented on a "Kingdom of God." Daniel presented his work as a product of the sixth century B.C. Babylonian exile, but it was actually a veiled attack on Syrian rule written four hundred years later. Ernst Bloch, a German Marxist theologian, maintains that Daniel became concerned with Jewish immortality, not due to a desire to prolong life but to secure eventual justice as a reversal of contemporary oppression: "The belief in a hereafter came to be one of the means to allay doubts about the justice of God on earth; above all, the very hope for a resurrection became a moral-juridical hope."[4]

During the Babylonian exile, Jewish messianism incorporated an apocalyptic eschatology which was further developed by Daniel and Enoch during the Greco-Syrian suzerainty. Apocalyptists, in contrast to earlier prophets, claimed to interpret the will of God from visions rather than revelations and stressed the awaited judgment by God rather than man's ability to repent.[5] Apocalypticism was based on the dualistic struggle between good and evil; on the coming of a messiah to eliminate the evil, and on the ending of an evil age and the establishment of an age of righteousness. Evil could not be expelled by man's action, only by the destructive capacity of God.

Messianic ideas were prevalent among the Jews during the first century B.C. as they did not have the power to free themselves from

Roman occupation; especially affected were the Essenes, a pietistic sect that strongly influenced Jesus and John the Baptist. John, a critic of immorality and believer in imminent judgment, predicted the coming of a messianic figure, usually interpreted as Jesus himself. According to David Aune, an expert on classics and religion, "John stands clearly in the apocalyptic tradition in that the judgment he envisions is not a historical judgment conceived as a divine punishment for specific transgressions, but an eschatological judgment regarded by John as the final and terrifying divine judicial response to the wickedness and corruption of Israel."[6] John, like Marx, pointed to revolution but did not bring it about. He wanted to prepare people for the Kingdom of God through purification of their hearts, but its advent had to await the messiah. The Kingdom of God would bring salvation to this world, but not be of it.[7] Whereas John readied himself for the Kingdom through spiritual retreat from earthly evils, Jesus confronted worldly tasks since he believed that man "must bear the future in the present."[8]

There were two messianic strands in Judaism, one applying to the establishment of an earthly kingdom and the other to a heavenly spiritual kingdom. The former was downplayed by later Christians, but paradoxically influenced the Romans in their decision to crucify Jesus.[9] The latter, derived from Ezekiel, the second Isaiah, Daniel and Enoch, gained a prominent place within Christianity through the Book of Revelation. However, many Christians believe that this spiritual Kingdom of God may actually occur on earth, and that Jesus envisioned it in a worldly context.

Echoing messianic prophesies of the period of Babylonian exile, Jesus often referred to himself as the "Son of Man." He was squarely in the Jewish tradition, but Christianity abruptly diverged when apostles called him the "Son of God" and the virgin birth, the incarnation and the Trinity were made centerpieces of Christian theology.

From the Apple to the Beast

The Book of Revelation, in the spirit of Old Testament messianism, is the most Jewish contribution to the New Testament as it appears to have been written earlier than other books and is not similarly influenced by Greco-Roman values.[10] Marxism, in the view of several scholars, is a secularized version of John's treatise, with Sovietologist Robert C. Tucker maintaining that Marx's *Das Kapital* is itself a Book of Revelation.[11]

Marxism and Christianity present messages of hope as man can rise from his fallen state and be redeemed. Nineteenth century evolutionary and progressive optimism thus merged with Christian theology to produce a blueprint for man's return to paradise achieved through the suffering of the proletariat. Everything occurring prior to the establishment of a classless society is "pre-history" as man proceeds through primitive communism, slavery, feudalism and capitalism toward his redemption in pure communism.

The cycle of human activity may be viewed as the fall from innocence in the Garden of Eden, expulsion from the Garden as a consequence of disobedience to God, the exile of the Jews into Egyptian slavery due to man's descent into contradictions, and the Exodus and return to the land of Israel as representative of liberation and redemption.[12] For Christians, the expectation of Christ's Second Coming leads to a complex scenario in which he returns to earth and destroys the ruling Anti-Christ in an apocalyptic confrontation, saints and martyrs are resurrected to join with Christ in reigning during the millenium (thousand year Kingdom of God), Satan becomes active following the millenium, everyone who has lived is resurrected to face the Last Judgment and there is the destruction of the world culminating, in some versions, in a final battle at Armageddon. This is the basic pre-millenial interpretation which places the parousia, or Second Coming, prior to the Kingdom of God. There is also a post-millenial school of thought which views the millenium as a transition to Christ's return.[13]

Marxism parallels Christianity in regard to man's fall, his preparation for the Kingdom of God, the coming of a messiah, the apocalyptic struggle and the advent of the millenium, with some scholars also discerning similarities to the Last Judgment. The theme of resurrection is not pertinent to Marxism, although the issue of immortality has been prominent among Soviet communists. Essentially, Marxism evokes those religions that are engaged in seeking their origins, returning to a lost paradise.[14] Historian James Scott appropriately remarks in regard to millenial religious ideologies:"While the earthly utopia is an anticipation of the future, it often harks back to a mythic Eden from which mankind has fallen away. It is no exaggeration to see in such historically common ideologies a revolutionary appropriation of religious symbolism in the service of class interests."[15]

Theologian Will Herberg observes a "triadic pattern" in which Marxism and Christianity go through a stage of harmony, justice and happiness; a second stage after leaving primitive communism or Eden of injustice and misery; and a third stage which features a return to the first. In both cases, the third stage is preceded by a final struggle against the bourgeoisie or Anti-Christ. Furthermore, Herberg relates this "triad" to Hegel's dialectic: the thesis is primitive communism or the Garden of Eden, the antithesis is class society or the fallen state of man, and the synthesis is communism or the millenium.[16]

Serpent in the Garden

Christians treat the act of creation as good, and don't believe that man's original sin is inherent in God's work. In the Garden of Eden, man quickly falls from grace due to his disobedience to God and becomes a sinner. Marxists concur with this interpretation of man's goodness at the creation but believe that the introduction of private property then produces exploitation and alienation. This Marxist parallel to the Christian concept of original sin fails, however, to explain why men began to claim the right to private property, basing such actions on apparent inevitability. Christians, on the other hand, see man as volitional and point to the sin of pride as the catalyst of acquisitiveness.[17]

More importantly, the Marxist version of the fall does not make each man responsible for sin. It is collective (in the Jewish tradition) rather than individual, societal rather than personal. The greed and profit inherent in private property reflect a corrupted social system so perfecting this system will eliminate sin and return man to his natural goodness. Many Christians therefore criticize Marxism for its deemphasis on individual moral responsibility and for its effort to save mankind, but not each particular man. Marxism, by not acknowledging individual guilt, is accused of insensitivity to ethical concerns as it is prepared to eliminate those who obstruct perceived historical progress.[18]

For Marxists, man retains his goodness even though he brought about his fall from grace. Society has sinned, and man is therefore capable of perfecting the world. The sinless proletariat, which has borne man's suffering, will achieve redemption; sin will be eliminated through societal transformation rather than love and forgiveness.[19] In this regard, Marxism retains the Jewish emphasis on man's ethical potential and rejects the Christian focus on man as sinner. So too does Marxism repudiate Christian dualism pertaining to the body and soul.

The Marxist account of the fall and redemption is related to the theme of alienation; man loses his innocence and comes into conflict with himself. Man is estranged and dehumanized, his being contradicting his existence.[20] Classes are also alienated from each other. Through the elimination of private property and classes, man may be redeemed from his alienation. For Christians, the forbidden fruit episode represents man's alienation from God, not from himself, and this may be overcome through forgiveness and the saving of man's soul.[21]

On Earth as it is in Heaven

Marxism, like Christianity, looks toward the triumph of good over evil. The conflict between them includes an inner dimension related to man's alienation and an outer one revolving around class conflict.[22] Belief in the ultimate victory of goodness incorporates apocalyptic and messianic themes similar to those of Christian pre-millenialists; evil, represented by the enmiseration of the working class, increases prior to salvation and the rise to power of the messianic proletariat takes place amidst a violent revolution.[23]

Communists and Christians see the future affecting the present as man prepares for the reign of justice. There is recognition of inward personal change, although the two movements diverge on the issue of human action. Atheistic communists stress inevitability, but assign a functional role to praxis; Christians attribute the advent of the Kingdom of God to divine intervention. Those Christians who share the Marxist (and Jewish) belief in praxis see man acting under God's inspiration; other Christians downplay the human contribution as people somewhat fatalistically await Christ's return.[24]

In the Marxist framework, the apocalypse signifies the defeat of evil and the inauguration of a just age, communism. Capitalism collapses through imperialist wars and the socialist revolution, and only then can man enter the classless society. The apocalypse is not linked to the destruction of the world, but to the commencement of a secular Kingdom of God. Property and sin are eliminated, and there is no need for state authority since man is good and his actions need not be constrained. Each receives according to his needs as man, rather than the grace of God, brings salvation.

Marxism is based on imminence rather than transcendence, on salvation within history ("And I am come down to deliver them out of the hand of the Egyptians, and to bring them up out of that land unto a good land and a large, unto a land flowing with milk and honey." - Exodus,

3:8) rather than from history. Its Kingdom of God replaces pre-history with history, and is definitely earthly rather than supernatural.[25] Although Christians are divided over the millenium's possible earthliness, there is an inherent transcendental and otherworldly character to the concept of martyrs and saints being resurrected.[26] Marxism also diverges from Christianity on the messianic impetus for the millenium. For the former, the proletariat symbolizes the first messianic coming; for the latter, Christs's reappearance on earth is seen as the Second Coming. Thus Marxism is more attuned to the Jewish tradition in which the messiah has not yet arrived. It also reflects the Jewish prophetic expectation of a messiah of the Davidic line establishing an earthly Kingdom of God.

Communism represents man's surmounting of history as he is no longer subject to an endless dialectic process.[27] In this sense, communism is not exactly a millenium as it lasts forever rather than being limited to a finite time span. Furthermore, Marxism is much more optimistic than Christianity as there is no Last Judgment which can condemn man to hell nor an Armageddon which can obliterate the earth.[28] The final end, or eschaton, of man's existence is the rather idyllic pure communism so that efforts to associate Marxism with the Last Judgment and Armageddon are misleading.[29] Scholars asserting such parallels refer to the collapse of capitalism, the socialist revolution and imperialist wars but Marxists assign these occurrences to the period leading up to the millenium, whereas Christians place the Last Judgment and Armageddon after the Kingdom of God.

Despite its materialism, Marxism incorporated numerous religious themes prevalent in nineteenth century European culture. Karl Marx underwent rigorous training in theology, and his Jewish background contributed to his psychological reaction to religious phenomena. Although avowedly atheist, Marx nevertheless dealt with concepts of messianism and redemption. Dialectical materialism therefore came to be imbued with Judaic and Christian content.

Notes

1. Jacques Maritain, *True Humanism*, sixth edition (London: Geoffrey Bles, 1954), p. 44; Milan Machovec, *A Marxist Looks at Jesus* (Philadelphia: Fortress Press, 1976), p. 193 and Mircea Eliade, *The Sacred and the Profane* (New York: Harcourt, Brace Jovanovich, 1959), p. 206. See also Jules Monnerot, *Sociology and Psychology of Communism* (Boston: Beacon Press, 1960), p. 39.
2. Christopher Dawson, *The Dynamics of World History* (New York: New American Library, 1962), p. 349.
3. See David Aune, *Prophesy in Early Christianity and the Ancient Mediterranean World* (Grand Rapids: William Eerdmans, 1983), p. 123 and Ernst Benz, *Evolution and Christian Hope* (Garden City: Doubleday, 1966), pp. 4-5.
4. Ernst Bloch, *Man on His Own* (New York: Herder and Herder, 1970), p. 94.
5. See Aune, pp. 111-14.
6. Aune, pp. 30-31. Although Aune considers John the Baptist to be an apocalypticist, he also points to John's emphasis on redemption through purification in the River Jordan.
7. Benz, p. 6.
8. Machovec, p. 91.
9. See Benz, pp. 1-4.
10. Friedrich Engels, "On the History of Early Christianity," in Lewis Feuer, ed., *Marx and Engels: Basic Writing on Politics and Philosophy* (Garden City: Doubleday, 1959), pp. 193-94.
11. Robert C. Tucker, *Philosophy and Myth in Karl Marx* (New York: Cambridge University Press, 1965), p. 231. See also Eduard Heimann, "Atheist Theocracy," *Social Research*, vol. 20, no. 3 (Fall, 1973):313; Nicholas Lash, *A Matter of Hope* (Notre Dame: University of Notre Dame Press, 1982), p. 51 and Eduard Heimann, *Reason and Faith in Modern Society* (Middletown, Connecticut: Wesleyan University Press, 1961), p. 157. Some analysts have compared Marx to St. Augustine. See Robert V. Daniels, *The Nature of Communism* (New York: Random House, 1962), p. 327 and Tucker, p. 22.
12. See James Adams, "Is Marx's Thought Relevant to the Christian?: A Protestant View," in Nicholas Lobkowicz, ed., *Marx and the Western World* (Notre Dame: University of Notre Dame Press, 1967), p. 381. Kenneth Murphy refers o the "imagined innocence and purity of Marx's socialist utopia." See *Retreat From the Finland Station* (New York: The Free Press, 1992), p. 380.
13. George Shepperson, "The Comparative Study of Millenarian Movements," in Sylvia Thrupp, ed., *Millennial Dreams in Action* (New York: Schocken, 1970), pp. 44-45. Some Christians relate the concept of the apocalypse to the end of the world, Armageddon.

14 See Thomas Altizer, "The Sacred and the Profane: A Dialectical Understanding of Christianity," in Thomas Altizer and William Hamilton, *Radical Theology and the Death of God* (Indianapolis: Bobbs-Merrill, 1966), p. 143.
15 James C. Scott, *Weapons of the Weak* (New Haven: Yale University Press, 1985), p. 332.
16 Will Herberg, *Faith Enacted as History* (Philadelphia: Westminster Press, 1976), pp. 181-84.
17 See Adams, p. 373; Karl Lowith, *Meaning in History* (Chicago: University of Chicago Press, 1949), p. 43 and William Hordern, *Christianity, Communism and History* (London: Lutterworth Press, 1957), p. 61.
18 See Lester DeKoster, *Communism and Christian Faith* (Grand Rapids: William Eerdmans, 1956), p. 44 and Czeslaw Milosz, *The Captive Mind* (New York: Vintage Books, 1951), pp. 199-200.
19 Mary DeVecchis, "Pessimism and Optimism in Communism," unpublished paper, pp. 2-3 and Gustav Wetter, *Dialectical Materialism* (New York: Praeger, 1958), p. 559.
20 Paul Tillich, *Political Expectation* (New York: Harper and Row, 1971), p. 91 and Paul Tillich, *The Protestant Era* (Chicago: University of Chicago Press, 1948), pp. 254-55.
21 M.B. Foster, "Historical Materialism," in D.M. Mackinnon, *Christian Faith and Communist Faith* (London: Macmillan, 1953), p. 95 and Yuri Furmanov, "Renewing Christ and Marx," *New Times*, no. 22 (May 29-June 4, 1990):30.
22 Louis Halle, "Marx's Religious Drama," *Encounter*, vol. XXV, no. 4 (October, 1965):37.
23 See Nicolas Berdyaev, *The Russian Revolution* (Ann Arbor: University of Michigan Press, 1966), p. 80.
24 Herndon Wagers, "Is Communism a Christian Heresy?," in Merrimon Cuninggim, ed., *Christianity and Communism* (Dallas: Southern Methodist University Press, 1958), pp. 80-81; Jacques Ellul, *The New Devils* (New York: Seabury Press, 1975), pp. 181-82; Dale Vree, *On Synthesizing Marxism and Christianity* (New York: John Wiley and Sons, 1976), p. 56; Hordern, pp. 78-79 and Peter Hebblethwaite, *The Christian-Marxist Dialogue* (New York: Paulist Press, 1977), pp. 114-15.
25 See Maritain, pp. 51-52.
26 For differing Christian interpretations, see Vree, pp. 37-41.
27 Maritain, p. 47.
28 S.F. Kissin describes Marxist "optimistic determinism." See *Farewell to Revolution* (New York: St. Martin's, 1978), p. 18.
29 See Arthur Koestler, *Arrow in the Blue* (New York: Macmillan, 1952), p. 280; Lowith, p. 44 and Crane Brinton, *Ideas and Men: The Story of Western Thought*, second edition (Englewood Cliffs: Prentice-Hall, 1963), p. 379.

Chapter IV

THE RELIGIOUS ATHEIST

Karl Marx denied the existence of God, but his eschatological and messianic visions had a strong religious component. Berdyaev was keenly observant in pointing out that the philosophy of history has a religious basis, either consciously or unconsciously, as it is in some ways a theology of history; Marx himself affirmed that he started with theological questions and turned them into questions about the world.[1] Surely Marx did not intend to create a religion, and he even warned that militant atheism could become a pseudo-religion.[2] Nevertheless, French political philosopher Regis Debray's remark that "iconoclasts only destroy the holy images they can replace" is highly pertinent to an evaluation of Marxism as a religion.[3]

Man and God

Marx rejected idealism and ideology but, in many ways, he was an idealist. While claiming that class determines consciousness, and that religious beliefs emanate from the superstructure, Marx lacked the proletarian background that should have produced his consciousness; his atheism provided the basis for his economic and sociological views, rather than vice-versa. Marx's belief in the inevitability of the proletarian mission preceded his development of historical materialism and, based on the intellectual evolution of his writings, he was clearly an atheist before he was a communist.[4] He was therefore an idealist, reminiscent of Hegel, as his explanation of phenomena evolved initially from spirit rather than matter.

Marx condemned ideology as a false consciousness constituting part of society's superstructure. Ideology was not seen as innate in human behavior, but was the product of alienation; it was a set of beliefs held by those who did not realize that their consciousness derived from materialism. Ideology was based on the values of the dominant economic class, and religions were defined as ideologies. If Marx's atheism was primordial and did not derive from materialism, he was not really an ideologue in accordance with Antoine Destutt de Tracy's conception of ideology (he is credited with originating this term) as the science of ideas which reflect the material base.

For Marx, religion was a form of false consciousness, an ideological illusion used to blur reality. It provided transitory happiness and made life bearable, serving as an opiate of the people masking the alienation evident in capitalist societies and substituting supernaturalism for dedication of energy to the revolutionary struggle of the proletariat. Religion represented the rejection of salvation on earth, emphasized metaphysics at the expense of reason, and degraded man through its anti-humanist interpretation of history.[5] According to Marx, religion would die out naturally once the material base of society changed; false consciousness would disappear during the transition to communism. There would be no role for religion once society had eliminated the alienations for which it served as a palliative.

Marx not only saw religion as an obstacle to the correction of society's faults but as a denigration of man ("Religion is only the illusory sun, which revolves round man as long as he does not revolve round himself." - *Toward the Critique of Hegel's Philosophy of Right*). Religion set forth its own vision of perfection in contrast to perceived human imperfection, and it denied that man could be his own savior.[6] Man lessened himself by attributing his best qualities to God and degraded himself before God, an image that he created. Influenced by Feuerbach, Marx placed man rather than God at the center of human activity and accentuated man's freedom by denying God as an instrument of control. Man deserved to be his own master, but his turn to religion indicated that he was not.[7] In the Marxist vision, man should be his own god, and his own savior; he must disengage himself from religion and discard his belief in God. Ultimately, as the dialectics of history unfold, he must be freed from himself and from the enslaving concepts of his creation.[8]

Marxism is atheistic, but nevertheless may be considered a religion.[9] Its rivalry with theological religions is indicative of some similarity, and its applied praxis ("Yea, a man may say, Thou hast faith, and I have works: show me thy faith without thy works and I will show thee my faith by my works." - James, 2:18) transforms its philosophy into a religion.[10]

Marxism unconsciously embodies attributes of both Judaism and Christianity and it seeks to change history, not just understand it. It incorporates moral hopes which are religious as they go beyond scientifically verifiable analysis; even its materialist interpretations are parallel to the Christian tradition. Marxism derives from Hegelianism, which is itself based on Christianity.

Marx retained the fundamental Christian concepts, but he left out God. He sought to eliminate alienation and achieve salvation through the termination of private property rather than through reunion with Him.[11] In the words of American Christian scholar Lester DeKoster: "Marx, in many ways, seems to have played the 'sedulous ape' to Christian doctrine, in each instance substituting the natural for the supernatural, the material for the spiritual, and the human for the Divine."[12]

Marxism, like religion, has a dualistic view of the world in which good combats evil, the exploited counter the exploiters. Overcoming societal evil and achieving salvation is a basic theme as man prepares for a new moral order and his own regeneration. This is a prophetic and eschatological approach, not a science of history, and it contains a sense of apocalyptic ethics in which the proletariat represents the triumph of good. Opponents of this inevitable evolutionary course are depicted as in sin as well as in error, and the ultimate goal of a classless society is inherently teleological and religious. Marxism strives for the sacred through the achievement of an ideal society and it bears a perceived absolute truth which will be the basis for a universality of values.[13]

Religion and the Dialectic

Jews point to the Covenant and the Exodus as indicative of God acting in history; Christians to the Incarnation which placed God on earth in human form; Marxists to a puposeful, dialectical materialist evolution. The latter has a strong teleological underpinning since reality is viewed as more than an accumulation of blind matter.[14] Marxism has an ingrained religiosity as matter progresses from less perfect to more perfect and becomes, in the words of German scholar Gustav Wetter, "a new absolute, a new divinity replacing the transcendent Creator-God." Dialectical materialism therefore produces "a sort of pseudo-Christianity" and "anti-church."[15] Its emphasis on the causal process likens it to the concept of natural law, but God becomes secularized as an omnipotent but impersonal force.[16] Dialectical materialism could be interpreted as metahistory, an examination of the causes and significance of historical change and the meaning and nature of history. This concept of metahistory parallels metaphysics, which deals with the causes of physical change, matter and the nature of being.[17]

The theme of alienation is highly germane to an evaluation of dialectical materialism as religion. Historian Owen Chadwick has argued that Marx's commentary on alienation would not have been possible in the absence of Jewish and Christian antecedents ("Then I looked on all the works that my hands had wrought, and on the labor that I had labored to do: and, behold, all was vanity and vexation of spirit, and there was no profit under the sun." - Ecclesiastes, 3:22) and prominent Christian theologians point out analogies to the fall and the Satanic force operating against man.[18] Alienation may be exhibited as idolatry. Psychoanalyst Erich Fromm somewhat controversially maintains that Old Testament prophets condemned idolatry less as a manifestation of worshiping several gods than as indicative of man worshiping, apart from himself, a product of his own labor ("They that make a graven image are all of them vanity; and their delectable things shall not profit; and they are their own witnesses; they see not, nor know; that they may be ashamed." - Isaiah, 44:9). This is similar to the idolatry perceived by Marx in the capitalist mode of production where idols are an alienated form of man's "life-forces."[19] Theologian Karl Lowith concurs with this latter point when he writes that Marx's atheism "is no longer a theological problem, i.e., a fight against heathen and Christian gods, but a fight against earthly idols. . . . The commodity-form of all our products is the new idol which has to be criticized and changed."[20]

At the heart of idol worship is money, described by theologian Mary Ruether in her critique of Marx as the wordly visible god, the "root expression of the golden calf." Money, for Marx, was "the empirical expression of this reification of man's self-alienation of his own creativity."[21] Marx condemned money for its corruptive and alienating effect, just as Jesus said that one cannot serve both God and Mammon.[22] But Marx's god was secular, the force leading to an earthly pure communist kingdom in which money was to be eliminated. All alienations were to be overcome as religion, ideology, the state and the family would all wither away.[23] Communism, according to Marx, would be "the transcendence of human self-estrangement;" through history, man would undergo a process of "coming-to-be" and giving birth to himself.[24]

Like the Jewish prophets, Marx refused to idolize objects or institutions but his perspective was atheistic as he turned against his Jewish heritage with both a practical and religious anti-Semitism.[25]

Nevertheless, he subconsciously incorporated Jewish concepts into his scholarly treatises and developed them into a Hebraicized, but secular, Christianity. Marxism later was reinterpreted and revised in the form of Leninism, which carried it further away from its Old Testament values toward the outlook and institutional edifices of medieval Christianity.

Notes

1. Nicolas Berdyaev, *The Origin of Russian Communism* (Ann Arbor: University of Michigan Press, 1960), p. 130 and Eugene Kamenka, *The Ethical Foundations of Marxism* (London: Routledge and Kegan Paul, 1962), p. 55.
2. Lester DeKoster, *Communism and Christian Faith* (Grand Rapids: William Eerdmans, 1956), p. 76 and Nicholas Lobkowicz, "Karl Marx's Attitude Toward Religion," *The Review of Politics*, no. 3 (July, 1964):352.
3. Regis Debray, *Critique of Political Reason* (London: NLB, 1983), p. 8.
4. Jacques Maritain, *True Humanism*, sixth edition (London: Geoffrey Bles, 1954), p. 46 and Nicolas Berdyaev, *The Russian Revolution* (Ann Arbor: University of Michigan Press, 1966), p. 81.
5. See J.M. Bochenski, "Marxism-Leninism and Religion," in Bohdan Bociurkiw and John Strong, eds., *Religion and Atheism in the U.S.S.R. and Eastern Europe* (Toronto: University of Toronto Press, 1975), p. 8.
6. See Berdyaev, *The Russian Revolution*, p. 28 and Debray, p. 223.
7. John Plamenatz, *Ideology* (New York: Praeger, 1970), p. 90; Maritain, p. 125 and Dale Vree, *On Synthesizing Marxism and Christianity* (New York: John Wiley and Sons, 1976), p. 125.
8. Mary DeVecchis, "Pessimism and Optimism in Communism," unpublished paper, p. 2 and Quentin Lauer, "The Atheism of Karl Marx," in Herbert Aptheker, ed., *Marxism and Christianity* (New York: Humanities Press, 1968), p. 54.
9. For citations that Marxism is a religion, see Eduard Heimann, "Atheist Theocracy," *Social Research*, vol. 20, no. 3 (Fall, 1973):312; S.F. Kissin, *Farewell to Revolution* (New York: St. Martin's, 1978), p. 49; Melvin Lasky, *Utopia and Revolution* (Chicago: University of Chicago Press, 1976), p. 62; Alfred Meyer, *Leninism* (New York: Praeger, 1957), p. 291; Jules Monnerot, *Sociology and Psychology of Communism* (Boston: Beacon Press, 1960), p. 123; Berdyaev, *The Origin of Russian Communism*, p. 100; Maritain, p. 28; DeKoster, p. 42; Joseph Schumpeter, *Capitalism, Socialism and Democracy*, third edition (New York: Harper and Row, 1950), p. 5; Trevor Ling, *Buddha, Marx, and God* (New York: St. Martin's, 1966), pp. 140-41 and Erich Fromm, *Beyond the Chains of Illusion* (New York: Simon and Schuster, 1962), p. 159. Aleksandr Yakovlev writes: In fact, Marxism's claim to be scientific is nothing other than a pseudoscientific new religion, which merely borrowed science's verbal attributes." See *The Fate of Marxism in Russia* (New Haven and London: Yale University Press, 1993), p. 102.
10. Ninian Smart, *In Search of Christianity* (San Francisco: Harper and Row, 1979), p. 143 and Monnerot, p. 123.
11. Jacques Ellul, *The New Demons* (New York: Seabury Press, 1975), p. 67; DeKoster, pp. 1-2 and 41; Reinhold Niebuhr, *Moral Man and Immoral Society* (New York: Charles Scribner's Sons, 1932), pp. 155-56 and John

Macmurray, "Christianity and Communism: Towards a Synthesis," in John Lewis, Karl Polanyi and Donald Kitchin, eds., *Christianity and the Social Revolution* (New York: Charles Scribner's Sons, 1936), pp. 508-509.

12 DeKoster, p. 41.

13 Howard Parsons, "The Prophetic Mission of Karl Marx," in Aptheker, p. 159; Christopher Dawson, *The Dynamics of World History* (New York: New American Library, 1962), p. 243; Schumpeter, p. 5; John Maynard, *The Russian Peasant and Other Stories* (New York: Collier Books, 1962), p. 476; Milovan Djilas, *The Unperfect Society: Beyond the New Class* (New York: Harcourt, Brace and World, 1969), p. 64; Harold Fallding, *The Sociology of Religion* (Toronto: McGraw-Hill Ryerson, 1974), p. 36; Giulio Girardi, *Marxism and Christianity* (New York: Macmillan, 1968), p. 194 and Niebuhr, p. 167. Political theorists Allan Bloom and David McLellan reject Marxism's religious credentials. Bloom is unwilling to treat atheism as a religion, and he similarly refuses to accept the concept of secularized Christianity. For him, religious experience cannot exclude God and it is inappropriate to use religious terminology to analyze values when philosophical terms are readily available. McLellan maintains that Marx was not a religious thinker, and that he was in fact highly anti-religious. He avers: "Marx's thought has an eschatological dimension which has strong religious roots. But a conception of the world can have a religious origin without itself being religious." Although Marx may have been influenced by Christian ideas, his position was clearly secular. See Allan Bloom, *The Closing of the American Mind* (New York: Simon and Schuster, 1987), pp. 210-11 and David McLellan, *Marxism and Religion* (New York: Harper and Row, 1987), Chapter One and pp. 159-61. See also Owen Chadwick, *The Secularization of the European Mind in the Nineteenth Century* (Cambridge: Cambridge University Press, 1975), p. 69. Both Bloom and McLellan make valid points as Marxism lacks common religious attributes such as belief in God and concern about an afterlife, and it obviously is secular. However, their remarks do not really contest the essence of Marxism as seen by scholars who deem it religious but instead are directed at semantic assumptions about religion. Those seeking an alternative explanation of Marxism's intrinsic nature should be directed toward the analysis of noted Sovietologist Robert C. Tucker, who claims that Marxism lacks ethical inquiry notwithstanding its consideration of good and evil. See *Philosophy and Myth in Karl Marx* (New York: Cambridge University Press, 1965), p. 16.

14 Arthur McGovern, *Marxism: An American Christian Perspective,* (Maryknoll, N.Y.: Orbis, 1980), p. 189; Dawson, p. 356 and Alban Widgery, *What Is Religion?* (New York: Harper and Brothers, 1953), p. 3.

15 Gustav Wetter, *Dialectical Materialism* (New York: Praeger, 1958), p. 558.

16 Heimann, p. 315 and Crane Brinton, *Ideas and Men: The Story of Western Thought*, second edition (Englewood Cliffs: Prentice-Hall, 1963), pp. 377-78. See also Maritain, p. 28; Arnold Toynbee, *A Study of History*,

Abridgement of Volumes I-VI (New York: Oxford University Press, 1946), p. 446 and William Hordern, *Christianity, Communism and History* (London: Lutterworth Press, 1957), p. 80.
17 For a discussion of metahistory, see Dawson, p. 281. See also John Marcus, *Heaven, Hell, and History* (New York: Macmillan, 1967), p. 172.
18 Chadwick, p. 68; Jan Milic Lochman, *Encountering Marx* (Philadelphia: Fortress Press, 1977), p. 69 and Joseph Petulla, *Christian Political Theology: A Marxian Guide* (Maryknoll. N.Y.: Orbis, 1972), p. 92.
19 Fromm, pp. 58-59.
20 Karl Lowith, *Meaning in History* (Chicago: University of Chicago Press, 1949), pp. 49-50.
21 Rosemary Ruether, *The Radical Kingdom* (New York: Harper and Row, 1970), p. 97.
22 See Lochman, p. 70.
23 See Parsons, p. 157.
24 Karl Marx, "Economic and Philosophical Manuscripts of 1844," in David Caute, ed., *Essential Writings of Karl Marx* (New York: Collier, 1970), pp. 223-24 and 227.
25 Sergei Bulgakov, *Karl Marx as a Religious Type* (Belmont, Massachusetts: Nordland, 1979), p. 96.

Chapter V

THE RUSSIFIED MISSION

Christianity, born in the land of Israel, spread through the Hellenized world before finding a permanent home in Rome; Marxism, child of the West European Industrial Revolution, was similarly repatriated by its adoption in agrarian Russia. Paradoxically, Marxism's appeal to the Russians was enhanced by its negative portrayal of Western capitalist societies - a depiction warmly received by those with somewhat xenophobic Slavophile tendencies.[1] So too did Marxism attract the intelligentsia in an economically backward country whose people, just emerging from serfdom, had experienced great suffering.[2]

As Marxism became woven into the Russian cultural fabric, its humanistic elements emblematic of the Enlightenment became overwhelmed by both inherent and societal authoritarian tendencies. Crane Brinton describes Marx's *Das Kapital* as presenting a complete cosmology of the "orthodox democratic tradition of the Enlightenment," and he discusses Marx's Enlightenment theme of "philosophical anarchism among free and equal human beings."[3] However, he recognizes Marx's concept of "the dictatorship of the proletariat" as contradictory to Enlightenment values and it was precisely this formulation that was accentuated by Lenin, who Russified Marxism by combining it with attributes of tsarist autocracy. Lenin carried out the socialist revolution and spread the communist gospel through the Second International and the Comintern, but he also institutionalized the party as a new clergy and established Bolshevik control in the form of a new church.

Cultural Receptivity

Bolshevism, like other movements based on faith, absorbed aspects of Russian culture in a syncretistic manner. It therefore embodied a great amount of traditionalism as there was, in the words of Berdyaev, "a Russification and orientalizing of Marxism."[4]

One of the evident underlying tenets of Bolshevism was the glorification of the common man as representative of universal truth. This harkens back to Slavophile images of the purity and simplicity of the peasant, or "muzhik," and the justice and righteousness that will be realized by his efforts.[5] Slavophiles, in common with later Bolsheviks, saw man fused with his community and they rejected individualism and materialism. They also had an absolutist sense of faith, which Berdyaev labels religious.[6] Russia was seen as morally superior to the West, and its suffering masses were alleged to possess an inherent energetic force that would lead mankind to salvation, illuminating in the process the "bourgeois darkness" of the West.[7]

Fundamental to Russian culture was the Christian theme of enduring suffering on the road to salvation, which may be likened to Marx's interpretation of the working class' enmiseration. Dostoyevsky's works provide ample evidence of this cultural trait, and former American communist Whittaker Chambers maintains that endless suffering was so accentuated that it appeared to be "a secret virtue."[8] Archbishop Fulton Sheen, an ardent foe of communism, recognizes the lasting impact of this observation: "Although it is hostile to Christianity, communism is using the 1000-year old Christian training of the Russian soul in the spirit of self-sacrifice and self-discipline. It is only because the shadow of Christ's Cross still falls across Russia that men are inspired to self-denial for a suprapersonal cause."[9] In fact, Russian Orthodox priests often portrayed the suffering under communist rule as divine retribution for the church's deviance from God's path. God wrought the October Revolution as a warning to the faithful as the church had sinned in not assisting the poor during the tsarist period. Sergei, who was then the Metropolitan of Moscow but later the Patriarch of the Russian Orthodox Church, declared: "We believe that the tribulation we experience is proof of the Orthodox Church's authenticity. Tribulation is evidence of the presence of Christ. . . . We are following Christ even in his suffering. . . . We believe that in our anguish Christ Himself is weeping and sweating and bleeding."[10]

Russian religious messianism included the expectation of an earthly Kingdom of God, which made atheistic Bolshevism more palatable to the masses. Bolshevism appealed to the sense of nihilism and ultimate salvation embedded in Russian culture, as well as to traditional Christian emphasis on Jesus' message being directed to the common man. As the Russian proletariat was so small, Bolshevism's appeal was significantly broadened by its identification with deeply implanted messianic elements.[11]

Sociologist Vatro Murvar argues that Russian Christian messianism influenced revolutionary messianism such as Bolshevism, which he accepts as a non-theistic religion. Both contain an absolutist sense of faith, an eschatological search for truth, moral austerity, anticipation of a millenium, and an apocalyptic vision of revolution leading to a Kingdom of God.[12] Sergei Bulgakov, who broke with Marxism and gained prominence as a Christian theologian, points out the possession by even atheistic members of the Russian intelligentsia of an eschatological image of the Kingdom of God and a tendency to blend religious and socialist concepts. Man (in a rather non-traditional Christian sense) was viewed as perfectible, and as capable of being his own savior. Bulgakov avers that the intelligentsia was imbued with religiousity and had an "unconscious longing" for Christ.[13]

Cultural historian James Billington discerns an apocalyptic component in Leninism which produces an interpretation of World War I as a global imperialist struggle featuring the demise of the Anti-Christ in the form of finance capital and the emergence of the true Christ through class warfare. Eventually there was to be a classless society as the millenium.[14] Chambers avers that Lenin's focus on world revolution was attuned to the redemptive spirit of the Russian people.[15]

Messianic groups in Russia accepted the principle of "sobornost," which subordinated individualism to group cohesion. Collectivist values, associated with the form of agricultural organization known as the "mir," predominated as unity and solidarity were emphasized and factionalism eschewed.[16] Such a perspective surely pervaded the communist period of rule, with historian of Bolshevism Rene Fueloep-Miller asserting: "The Russian has never been able to perceive the ultimate development of humanity except in a collective form, in a conception of the collectivity, of the 'people,' into which even the Russian idea of God has always been retransformed."[17]

Bolshevik Apostles

Just as Christians adapted Judaism to the Roman Empire, Lenin revised Marxism to make it conform to the realities of tsarist Russia. As capitalism was in its infancy, Lenin maintained that the socialist revolution would take place at the weakest link in the capitalist chain rather than where it was most fully developed; as the proletariat was miniscule due to the low level of industrialization, Lenin deemed the peasantry a revolutionary force that would align with the workers; and as the workers lacked the political consciousness necessary to carry out a revolution, a communist party was required to serve as the vanguard. Lenin did not share Marx's historical faith, relying instead on organizing a revolutionary party, delineating its tactics, and acting whenever the moment was opportune. The party leaders became "the creators of history" as spontaneity and determinism were subordinated to voluntarism.[18] Ninian Smart, a professor of religion, points out that the New Testament became more important liturgically than the Old because it was distinctively Christian.[19] So too with Leninism as it superseded Marxism within the communist movement.

Lenin was an atheist but it is important to realize that his father regularly attended Orthodox services, his mother occasionally took part in Orthodox and Lutheran services, and he was married to Nadezhda Krupskaya in an Orthodox wedding ceremony. Lenin also studied religion in high school.[20] To what degree he may have been influenced by Christianity is dificult to determine, but he certainly absorbed at least subconsciously the New Testament undercurrents in Marxism. Russian writer Maxim Gorky, who was close to Lenin, calls attention to Bolshevism's religious roots and historian John Maynard discerns parallels between the practices of the Orthodox Church and the communist party. He sees both as congregationalist since a member may be separated from his brethren as a punishment, but restored to good standing after the confession of sin.[21]

It was not unusual for Christianity to become blended with socialism in late nineteenth century Russia, producing an overtly secular revolutionary ideology with strong religious overtones. Moral judgments derived from Christian faith, and socialism was often portrayed as a religion. The Socialist Revolutionaries proclaimed May Day of 1901 as the holiday of this religion, labeled Jesus the first socialist preacher, and issued "A New Sermon on the Mount" on May Day of 1905. The following year, a tract called "Ten Commandments of a Social Democrat" was published.[22] After the Bolsheviks came to power in 1917, Andrei Bely wrote a poem praising the revolution entitled "Christ is Resurrected," while Aleksandr Blok's poem "The Twelve" had an invisible Christ leading the revolutionaries.[23]

Bolshevism was similar to Sectarianism, a conglomeration of mystical Old Believer groups that split off from Orthodoxy beginning in 1666 plus denominations of non-Russian origin such as the Baptists and Jehovah's Witnesses. In fact, Fueloep-Miller goes so far as to claim that Leninism was actually Sectarianism cloaked in Marxist ideology as a means of concealing its religious nature.[24] Murvar has a differing perspective in which Bolshevism gained public acceptance because of its appeal to the Sectarian beliefs of the people, who viewed the corrupt tsarist system as the Anti-Christ.[25] The Sectarians sought earthly salvation, stressed equality, opposed serfdom, and rejected private property. They believed that property would negate the spiritual struggle against the Anti-Christ and delay the millenium as man would become too materialistic.[26] Their views surely helped predispose Russia to socialist values.

Such beliefs were well known to Lenin through his close association with Vladimir Bonch-Bruevich, a founding member of the Russian Social Democratic Labor Party to which Lenin also belonged. Bonch-Bruevich worked for a Christian socialist journal and traveled to Canada in 1899 with a Sectarian group known as the Dukhobors prior to his affiliation with Lenin in the publication of the newspaper *Iskra* (The Spark). At the R.S.D.L.P. congress of 1903, where the party split into Bolshevik and Menshevik wings, Lenin introduced a resolution based on a paper prepared by Bonch-Bruevich. The latter was anxious to have the Bolsheviks make a special appeal to the Sectarians, whom he viewed as peasants poised to become proletarians. Bonch-Bruevich maintained that Sectarians were collectivist and millenarian, and hoped to defeat the tsarist Anti-Christ in preparation for an earthly Kingdom of God. He advised that the groups most susceptible to Bolshevik entreaties were the Dukhobors and Khlysty, both mystical sects, as well as the Jehovah's Witnesses and Neo-Shtundists. Lenin's resolution was approved, and Bonch-Bruevich was authorized to publish a journal directed at the Sectarians. Nine issues of *Rassvet* (Dawn) were issued from January through September 1904 in which the Bolsheviks called upon the Sectarians to turn from religious protest to political action.[27] As will be seen, Lenin's relationship with Bonch-Bruevich was to be enduring, and Bonch-Bruevich maintained his special interest in Sectarian communities.

In addition to Bronch-Bruevich, a linkage between the communist revolutionaries and Christianity was provided by Marxists known as the "God-seekers." They called for man to perfect himself morally in preparation for political and social change; their emphasis on spirit rather than matter led them to shift away from Marxism during the period 1900-1902 and break with it completely after the working class' failures during the 1905 attempt at revolution. Most prominent among the "God-seekers" were Nicolas Berdyaev, a philosopher who later wrote influential accounts of Bolshevism's resemblance to religion, and Sergei Bulgakov, who became a religious scholar and priest.[28]

Leninism incorporated Russian Christian concepts related to the "Third Rome" and the sanctity of the Kremlin. The "Third Rome" tradition was strong within the Russian culture as Moscow was seen as the heir to Rome, which fell to barbarians, and to Constantinople, which was taken over by the Moslems. Many members of the Orthodox faith believed that the Second Coming would take place in the Kremlin, which was revered as a holy site, and sociologist Christel Lane says that she knows Russian expatriots who wear packets of Kremlin soil over their hearts.[29] It was not fortuitous that when the capital had to be moved from Petrograd for security reasons, Lenin chose Moscow as its new location and the Kremlin, with its religious overtones, was selected as the seat of power. Symbolically, this represented a withdrawal from Europe - forsaking cosmopolitan Petrograd, Peter the Great's opening to the West, for Moscow, the historic and spiritual focus of the heartland.[30] Holy Russia was to serve as a barrier against perceived reactionaries or, in the words of writer Arthur Koestler, a "mental defense of a creed against the foreign intervention of doubt." Koestler maintained that "progress had recovered its lost religion" as the Soviet system became a new opiate.[31] Lenin, the atheistic Marxist, thus established a communist hegemony that echoed his own depiction of religion, an ideological legitimization of class rule.[32]

Crane Brinton describes Paul as an administrator, theologian and universalizer of the church.[33] Such attributes apply to Lenin as well, but he also resembles Constantine in introducung an external doctrine that soon became the state religion. Lenin was unlike Jesus in this regard, but his messianic revolutionary role and early death led many to deify him as a communist Christ.

In His Own Image

The most significant religious impact upon Bolshevism was furnished by the "God-builders," who consciously fused their theological concepts with Marxism.[34] Representing the less rationalist wing of Lenin's party, they sought to develop socialism more as a religion than as a science and they depicted Marx as a prophet. In essence, they wanted religion without God and hoped to establish a spiritual sense of community through the periodic staging of public festivals. "God-building" had much in common with the utopian vision of Tommaso Campanella, a Catholic theorist who published *City of the Sun* in 1602. In it, he described a city where statues of dead heroes abounded and whose walls were inscribed with scientific laws. The writer Maxim Gorky is known to have brought Campanella's work to the attention of both Lenin and the prime theorist of "God-building," Anatoly Lunacharsky.[35]

Associated with "God-building" were the Bolsheviks Aleksandr Bogdanov, Leonid Krassin and Lunacharsky, as well as Gorky who had a lengthy friendship with Lenin but never officially joined the party. Bogdanov and Lunacharsky were brothers-in-law, and both Lunacharsky and Gorky wrote for *Vpered* (Forward), a St. Petersburg newspaper edited by Lenin in late 1905. Krassin organized Gorky's April 1906 American tour, an effort to raise funds for the Bolsheviks, and may have helped recruit students for a school Gorky was establishing in Italy.[36] Krassin was a lesser figure at this time among the "God-builders," but his significant role following Lenin's death will be discussed later.

Lenin was not a "God-builder," but he had considerable interaction with the movement. In the spring of 1905, he sent Bonch-Bruevich as an emissary to Gorky to request that income from his books, and those of other authors published abroad, be channeled to Bolshevik coffers.[37] Beginning in October 1906, Gorky began to spend most of his time in Capri, Italy but he and Lenin did meet in London in 1907. Gorky's efforts to open a "God-building" school in Capri drove a conceptual wedge between the two men, which resulted in institutional rivalry. Gorky, together with Lunacharsky and Bogdanov, operated the Capri school only from August through December of 1909. The students were workers from Russia, and their number probably never exceeded eighteen. Lenin vehemently objected to the curriculum and encouraged five of the

Capri students to defect to his own school in Paris. The "God-building" endeavor in Capri was short-lived due to this internal dissension, but Gorky and Lunacharsky did offer a similar curriculum in Bologna from November 1910 through March 1911. Lenin and Gorky maintained a stormy but friendly relationship until Lenin's death in 1924, and Lenin made an important visit of reconciliation to Capri in 1910.

Anatoly Lunacharsky was the main theorist of "God-building," especially via his 1908 book *Religion and Socialism*. He saw Marxism as an anti-metaphysical, scientific and human religion derived from Judaism, and he called it "the most religious of all religions."[38] For him, religion was a "necessary illusion" that provides a crucial spiritual bond among men and inspires human achievement. In Lunacharsky's anti-rationalist interpretation, religion serves man's emotional needs and permits him to change the world, not just analyze it.[39] It will not wither away.

Lunacharsky excluded God from his presentation, averring: "Man does not need God, he himself is God. Man is a God to man."[40] External gods humiliate man, and collective immortality may only be achieved by elevating man to divinity. Mankind is deified and the evolution of the human spirit proceeds worldwide toward a "universal soul."[41] Lunacharsky wanted Bolshevism to pattern itself after religion in order to fulfill man's spiritual needs.

Aleksandr Bogdanov concurred on the religiosity of Marxism and stressed the god-like nature of the collective. However, his main focus was not really religion but philosophy. In this regard, he deviated from Marx's materialism in arguing that ideas enable man to create his own reality and materialism only exists when perceived by man's senses. Consciousness influences society's material base. Interestingly, Bogdanov's father was a priest and his chosen revolutionary pseudonym (the original family name was Malinovsky) means "given by God."[42]

Gorky, although not technically a Bolshevik, contributed to "God-building" through his courses at Capri and his books such as *Mother* (1907) and *Confession* (1908). He opposed established churches and called for a humanistic religion based upon the absolute perfection of man's mind. In a letter to Tolstoy, Gorky stated that "man is a depository of the living God. By God I understand one's untamable yearning for self-perfection, for truth and justice. . . . I deeply believe that there is nothing better than man on earth . . . I have always been and shall always be a man-worshipper."[43] According to Israeli Sovietologist Mikhail Agursky, Gorky's favorite book in the Bible was Job as man is portrayed as equal to God rather than enslaved by Him.[44]

Lenin railed against Gorky's views, charging that any justification of the concept of god contributes to reaction and that "God-building" is "ideological necrophilia." The idea of god "always tied down the oppressed classes with a faith in the divine character of the oppressors."[45] Lenin condemned Gorky's *Confession*, and lambasted "God-building" in his 1908 work *Materialism and Empiriocriticism*. He was particularly concerned about "God-building's" underlying idealism as it rejected materialism as the basis of ideas and implied some higher force leading toward perfectibility.[46] Lenin denied that "god is a complex of ideas that awaken and organize social feelings" and saw the concept of god as an opiate of the class struggle. He also felt that the "God-builders" paid insufficient attention to man's "deeds," concentrating instead on "self-contemplation" and "self-admiration."[47] Lenin's differences with Gorky were philosophical, but the related practical issue of how the party should appeal to the masses was also crucial.

Lenin agreed with his Marxist political foe Georgy Plekhanov on the essence of the "God-builders." Plekhanov had written: "They start out by declaring God a fiction, and end by proclaiming man a god. But since humanity is not a fiction, why call it a god? Why should it be regarded flattering for humanity to be identified with one of his own fictions?"[48] In fact, Lenin was so outraged by "God-building" that he expelled Bogdanov and Lunacharsky from the Bolshevik party in June 1909. In all fairness, it must be added that Bogdanov had also incurred Lenin's wrath by opposing his call for Bolshevik participation in the Russian legislature, or Duma. Once the revolutionary events of 1917 unfolded, Bogdanov and Lunacharsky returned to the party and led a resurgence of "God-building" that had a profound impact upon the Soviet system. They were joined by Gorky and Krassin as Lenin, the iconoclast, became deified as a man-god upon his death.[49]

Notes

1. See Arnold Toynbee, *A Study of History*, abridgement of volumes I-VI (New York: Oxford University Press, 1946), p. 204.
2. See Yevgeny Yevtushenko, *A Precocious Autobiography* (London: Collins and Harvill, 1963), pp. 37-39.
3. Crane Brinton, *Ideas and Men: The Story of Western Thought*, second edition (Englewood Cliffs: Prentice-Hall, 1963), pp. 374 and 381. See also Vatro Murvar, "Messianism in Russia: Religious and Revolutionary," *Journal for the Scientific Study of Religion*, vol. 10, no. 4 (Winter, 1971):306.
4. Robert V. Daniels, *The Nature of Communism* (New York: Random House, 1962), p. 350 and Nicolas Berdyaev, *The Origin of Russian Communism* (Ann Arbor: University of Michigan Press, 1960), p. 107.
5. See Whittaker Chambers, *Cold Friday* (New York: Random House, 1964), p. 173.
6. Dinko Tomasic, *The Impact of Russian Culture on Soviet Communism* (Glencoe: Free Press, 1953), p. 124 and Berdyaev, p. 21.
7. Chambers, p. 181 and Nicolas Berdyaev, *The Russian Revolution* (Ann Arbor: University of Michigan Press, 1966), p. 72.
8. Chambers, p. 178.
9. Fulton Sheen, *Communism and the Conscience of the West* (Indianapolis: Bobbs-Merrill, 1948), p. 192.
10. Pierre Van Paassen, *Visions Rise and Change* (New York: Dial Press, 1955), pp. 70-71 and 154-55.
11. See Berdyaev, *The Russian Revolution*, p. 72; Van Paassen, p. 258; Berdyaev, *The Origin of Russian Communism*, pp. 8 and 106; Nicholas Vakar, *The Taproot of Soviet Society* (New York: Harper and Brothers, 1961), p. 11 and John Maynard, *The Russian Peasant and Other Stories* (New York: Collier Books, 1962), p. 476. For a discussion of messianic aspects of nineteenth century Russian nationalism, see Hans Kohn, "Dostoyevsky and Danilevsky: Nationalist Messianism," in Ernest Simmons, ed., *Continuity and Change in Russian and Soviet Thought* (Cambridge: Harvard University Press, 1955), pp. 500-515.
12. Murvar, pp. 280 and 283-85.
13. James Pain and Nicolas Zernov, *A Bulgakov Anthology* (Philadelphia: Westminster Press, 1976), pp. 51-53. Julian Towster has written: "Russian thought was ever concerned with the meaning of history, its ultimate end, the nature of man and his role and fate in history. The Russian thinkers produced great theodicies of history charged with moralisms and permeated with the conviction that moral purpose was the dynamo of the social scene." See "Vyshinsky's Concept of Collectivity," in Simmons, p. 240.
14. James Billington, *Fire in the Minds of Men* (New York: Basic Books, 1980), p. 466.
15. Chambers, pp. 190-91.

16 Murvar, p. 319 and Rene Fueloep-Miller, *The Mind and Face of Bolshevism* (New York: Harper and Row, 1965), p. 8.
17 Fueloep-Miller, p. 7.
18 See Dale Vree, *On Synthesizing Marxism and Christianity* (New York: John Wiley and Sons, 1976), p. 137.
19 Ninian Smart, *In Search of Christianity* (San Francisco: Harper and Row, 1979), p. 222.
20 Bohdan Bociurkiw, "Lenin and Religion," in Leonard Schapiro and Peter Reddaway, eds., *Lenin: The Man, the Theorist, the Leader* (New York: Praeger, 1967), p. 110.
21 Mikhail Agursky, "Maksim Gorky and the Decline of Bolshevik Theomachy," in Nicolai Petro, ed., *Christianity and Russian Culture in Soviet Society* (Boulder: Westview, 1990), p. 69 and Maynard, p. 475.
22 Richard Stites, *Revolutionary Dreams* (New York: Oxford University Press, 1989), pp. 102-104 and Berdyaev, *The Russian Revolution*, pp. 8-9.
23 See Mikhail Agursky, *The Third Rome: National Bolshevism in the USSR* (Boulder: Westview, 1987), pp. 172 and 175.
24 Fueloep-Miller, p. 88. The Old Believers represented a revolt of the parish priests against the central Orthodox church authorities, thus exhibiting a form of class antagonism also found in Bolshevism.
25 Murvar, p. 300.
26 Tomasic, p. 156; Murvar, pp. 298-99 and Fueloep-Miller, pp. 74-75.
27 Murvar, pp. 299-300; Nina Tumarkin, *Lenin Lives! The Lenin Cult in Soviet Russia* (Cambridge: Harvard University Press, 1983), p. 19 and Bociurkiw, pp. 114-15.
28 According to Bulgakov, he discarded Marxism because it was too Western and he came to view socialism as a punishment for the sins of indifference to religion while professing piety and of insufficient social concern. See Pain and Zernov, and Alexander Kaun, *Maxim Gorky and His Russia* (New York: Benjamin Blom, 1931), p. 414. See also George Putnam, *Russian Alternatives to Marxism* (Knoxville: University of Tennessee Press, 1977).
29 Christel Lane, *The Rites of Rulers* (Cambridge: Cambridge University Press, 1981), p. 127. See also Chambers, p. 165.
30 See Hans Kohn, *The Mind of Modern Russia* (New York: Harper and Brothers, 1955), pp. 32-33.
31 Arthur Koestler, *The Yogi and the Commissar* (New York: Macmillan, 1945), p. 117.
32 Matthew Spinka, *Christianity Confronts Communism* (New York: Harper and Brothers, 1936), p. 162.
33 Brinton, p. 112.
34 Joseph Dietzgen, a German who lived in Russia and the United States during the nineteenth century, was an intellectual predecessor of the "God-builders." So were Ludwig Feuerbach and Auguste Comte. See Julius Hecker, *Moscow Dialogues* (London: Chapman and Hall, 1933), pp. 197-98 and Agursky, *The Third Rome*, p. 88.

35 Bociurkiw, p. 122 and Stites, pp. 88 and 98.
36 Kaun, pp. 370-71, 393 and 569. For an analysis of the views of the *Vpered* group, see Agursky, *The Third Rome*, pp. 82-92.
37 Agursky, *The Third Rome*, p. 368.
38 Bertram Wolfe, *Three Who Made a Revolution* (Boston: Beacon Press, 1948), p. 506; Thomas Masaryk, *The Spirit of Russia*, vol. II (London: Allen and Unwin, 1919), p. 359 and George Kline, *Religious and Anti-Religious Thought in Russia* (Chicago: University of Chicago Press, 1968), p. 122.
39 Dan Levin, *Stormy Petrel: The Life and Work of Maxim Gorky* (New York: Appleton-Century, 1965), pp. 3-4.
40 Robert Williams, "Collective Immortality: the Syndicalist Origins of Proletarian Culture, 1905-1910," *Slavic Review*, vol. 39, no. 3 (September, 1980):393.
41 See Stites, p. l02.
42 Williams, p. 391; James McClelland, "Utopianism Versus Revolutionary Heroism in Bolshevik Policy: The Proletarian Culture Debate," *Slavic Review*, vol. 39, no. 3 (September, 1980):413 and Levin, pp. 153-54.
43 Kaun, pp. 295-96.
44 Agursky, "Maksim Gorky," p. 90.
45 Kaun, pp. 437-38 and Bociurkiw, pp. l09 and 123. See also Bertram Wolfe, *The Bridge and the Abyss* (New York: Praeger, 1967), pp. 50-51.
46 See Fueloep-Miller, pp. 50-51.
47 Kaun, pp. 438 and 440.
48 Kaun, p. 418.
49 See Tumarkin, p. 23.

Chapter VI

BOLSHEVIK ON THE CROSS

Lenin represented the Christianization of Marxism, the messianic leader who would lead his people toward a secular Kingdom of God.¹ Parallels with Jesus are abundant as Lenin served as the savior of the downtrodden proletariat, suffered through three strokes brought on in part by the wounds received in a political assassination attempt, died prematurely and was then embalmed by his followers in an effort to transcend death. He was deified as a communist Christ, and his mausoleum adjacent to the Kremlin wall became a place of religious reverence. How ironic an ending for the strident foe of "God-building!"

The Living Icon

Rene Fueloep-Miller reports that Russian peasants described Lenin in Biblical terms.² Orthodoxy was steeped in messianic tradition, and religious interpretations were pervasive within the Russian culture. Even the Bolsheviks had their "God-builders" such as Lunacharsky, who evidently was inspired to a state of spiritual encomium when he wrote: "The structure of Vladimir Ilyich's skull is truly striking. One has to study him for a little while and then instead of the first impression of a plain, large, bald head one begins to appreciate the physical power, the outlines of the colossal dome of his forehead, and to sense something which I can only describe as a physical emanation of light from its surface."³

On August 30, 1918, Lenin was seriously wounded by gunfire, but survived. This event had the effect of galvanizing religious sentiments, leading even the atheistic Bolshevik official Grigory Zinoviev to call Lenin an "apostle" and to proclaim that "he is the leader by the grace of God." Other reactions to the assassination attempt were also rich in Christian symbolism.[4] Lenin told Bonch-Bruevich and several associates that he wanted a halt to the development of a personality cult, and he attacked an article by Gorky which was overly adulatory.[5] He additionally criticized the extensive attention lavished upon him in April 1920 on the occasion of his fiftieth birthday.

As Lenin's health declined, a devotional cult claimed that he was indeed robust. Furthermore, the term "Leninism" was coined in an effort to elevate his pronouncements; the communist party newspaper *Pravda*, in a passage imbued with Christianity, declared: "Lenin is the suffering for an idea; it is bleeding for the proletariat."[6] In July 1923, a Lenin Institute was established to study his thought and, the following month, an economic exhibition included a "Lenin corner" filled with memorabilia which could be perused by visiting peasants. It was arranged similarly to icon corners in their homes.[7] The eulogizing of Lenin had begun, but he was still clinging to life.

Death and Life

Lenin died on January 21, 1924. His body was then temporarily embalmed to last for six days, and then embalmed again for another forty days. Lenin lay in state in the Hall of Columns, which was decorated with palm branches that were often used to symbolize Christ's martyrdom. On January 27, following his funeral, Lenin's body was placed in a wooden mausoleum in Red Square.[8]

Although Lenin's funeral included no prayers or quasi-Christian rituals, the period of his death was marked by a religiosity that elevated the departed Vladimir Ilyich to the status of sainthood and, in the eyes of many, a second Jesus Christ. Zinoviev labeled him a "prophet," and Stalin eulogized him in a January 26 oration that bore great similarity to the Orthodox style of prayer.[9] On the day of the funeral, Lunacharsky called Lenin the creator and martyr of a new communist world. He declared: "We have seen Man, Man with a capital letter."[10] His fellow "God-builder" Maxim Gorky used an almost identical phrase, "a Man with a capital M," and he seemed to be making an analogy to Jesus when he talked about the "heroism of a man who has renounced all the joys of earth for the sake of the difficult labor for the happiness of men."[11]

Historians Louis Fischer and Isaac Deutscher maintain that the communists, either consciously or unconsciously, used Lenin's death to appeal to the religious proclivities of the people, and there was a catharsis which released the communists from adherence to strict Marxist materialism.[12] Death generally taps primordial spiritual roots, and even the communist party's statement the day after Lenin's demise had overtones of the bread and wine in the Holy Eucharist ("Then Jesus said unto them, Verily, verily, I say unto you, Except ye eat the flesh of the Son of man, and drink his blood, ye have no life in you." - John, 6:53). It asserted: "Lenin is dead, but he lives in the soul of each one of the members of the Party. Each member of the Party is a portion of Lenin. Our whole Communist family is the collective incarnation of Lenin."[13] The party also popularized the slogan, with its obvious allusions to Christ, of "Lenin lived; Lenin lives; Lenin shall live." Descriptions of Lenin offered by school children frequently had Christian themes, and women dedicated prayer candles and said mass for him.[14] Bonch-Bruevich wrote that the movement of the working masses was led by Lenin after his physical death.[15]

Religious devotion to Lenin was in part spontaneous and derivative of the Orthodox culture, but there was surely an element of elite manipulation and cynicism which has led historian Nina Tumarkin to claim that the Lenin cult featured the use of religious imagery for political purposes.[16] Iconizing an individual creates a mythical quality and an image of order and stability in the face of a leader's death; it also grants religious status to the surviving party compatriots, turning them into apostles chosen to continue his mission.[17] French philosopher and government adviser Regis Debray observes that the deaths of Lenin and Jesus contributed to group organization. Death "introduces value" and represents "potential apotheosis." Debray continues: "Since it is the basis of the group unconscious and the source of group history, death is present in all foundation myths."[18]

Beyond the Flesh

The question of embalming Lenin came up in the late fall of 1923 while he was still alive. At a Politburo meeting, Stalin is alleged to have said that the Russian tradition was at variance with cremation and that some unnamed comrades in the provinces rejected it on that basis. He therefore recommended embalming upon Lenin's death, but met opposition from Nikolai Bukharin and Lev Kamenev.[19] Once Lenin did expire, Bonch-Bruevich played a key role in planning the funeral arrangements. Along with Lenin's widow Krupskaya and Lenin's two sisters and brother, he did not agree to embalming but the countervailing view of Stalin, Zinoviev and Lunacharsky won out. Crucial to this decision was the role of Leonid Krassin, a "God-builder," who was an engineer and a member of the funeral commission (Lunacharsky and Bonch-Bruevich were also members, but Stalin was not). He believed that science could eventually make resurrection possible, and he supervised the embalming process and installed a refrigeration system to preserve Lenin's body. It did not work properly and further embalming became necessary in March 1924.[20] When Krupskaya died in February 1939, she was cremated and the urn was placed in Lenin's mausoleum for her funeral and then buried near the Kremlin wall.[21]

The Orthodox tradition often included preservation of the intact bodies of saints, as contrasted with Catholic practice which retained parts of a body as holy relics. It was believed that they would not decompose, leading the communists to dig up such corpses in order to demonstrate decay and disprove saintly claims. George Bernard Shaw visited an anti-religious museum in Leningrad where a guide from the League of the Militant Godless showed him the undecayed bodies of two peasants, thereby attempting to undermine the Orthodox contention that only bodies of saints could be preserved in such a manner. Shaw cynically inquired how she knew that these two peasants were not saints.[22]

Following an autopsy, Lenin's heart and brain were sent to the Lenin Institute for study and his brain was preserved. The Orthodox had sometimes preserved the hearts of saints as relics; in this case, Lenin's brain received similar treatment.[23] Thus Vladimir Ilyich was embalmed, and a relic from his body was kept for posterity. In the words of his friend and biographer Louis Fischer: "The iconoclast is now a modern Russian icon, and millions queue and gaze in wonder at the miracle of his preservation in the flesh."[24]

The embalming of Lenin had strong overtones of immortality. Religions often deal with this issue through concepts of reincarnation, an afterlife, or communion with the spirits of ancestors. Christianity is especially "death-defying" as it includes the prospect of heaven and stresses the overcoming of death through Christ's resurrection. Lenin's immortalization, as represented by embalming and the construction of an elaborate mausoleum, was attuned to his culture's Orthodoxy and was at variance with "death-accepting" beliefs evident in Judaism.[25] The burial place of Moses was modest and secret as idolization of the dead was to be avoided. So too was the notion of an afterlife deemphasized in Jewish thought, and resurrection not affirmed. Thus Karl Marx's entombment may be linked to the Jewish tradition based on the finiteness of life, while Lenin's exhibited characteristics more consistent with Christianity. Marx was buried in a simple plot in London's Highgate Cemetery, and his grave never became a place of religious reverence. Although the site was moved in 1956 and adorned with a sculpted bust of Marx, it is still far from being a shrine as upkeep is financed through the sale of Karl Marx coffee mugs and rights sold to commercial entrepreneurs. On one occasion, an Italian sportswear company promoting clothes with Cyrillic lettering received permission to pose its models in front of Marx's tomb.[26]

Orthodoxy in Russia emphasized the theme of Easter and resurrection, and there was a widespread belief in the medical community that the dead could eventually be restored to life. The "God-builders" developed this viewpoint, with Bogdanov asserting that physical immortality could be approached through blood transfusions as the normal human life span could be extended to 100-120 years. Using technology in order to cheat death was an important "God-building" theme, and it fit in well with communism's vision of man mastering history through his intellect and triumphing over time.[27] Gorky proclaimed: "The human mind declares war on death as a natural phenomenon. On death itself. My personal belief is that sooner or later, probably in two hundred years or possibly one hundred years, man will indeed achieve immortality." He added that it would be done without the assistance of God.[28] Bogdanov opened an Institute for Blood Transfusions in Moscow and performed six transfusions successfully. On his seventh effort in April 1928, he exchanged his own blood with that of a student known to have malaria and tuberculosis. Bogdanov seemed to have realized correctly that the experiment would result in his own death.[29]

Deification

Lenin's body was first placed in a mausoleum in Red Square. An improved wooden version was completed four months later and, in

November 1924, plans were initiated to construct a permanent tomb. Lunacharsky was put in charge of a design competition, and Krassin spoke before the Immortalization Commission (the renamed funeral commission) that supervised the project. A proposal from A.V. Shchusev, an architect experienced in building Orthodox churches, was selected and it led to the building of a granite structure resembling the stepped pyramid tombs of ancient Egypt. This new mausoleum was opened in November 1930 and housed Lenin's body until July 1941 when the exigencies of war necessitated the relocation of Vladimir Ilyich to Tiumen in Western Siberia. A sarcophagus containing his embalmed remains was placed in a former school building, and returned to the Red Square mausoleum in April 1945.[30]

Krupskaya opposed the construction of a mausoleum, and her open letter on the subject appeared in *Pravda* nine days after Lenin's death. In it, she pleaded: "Do not permit your grief for Ilyich to take the form of external reverence for his person. Do not raise memorials to him, palaces named after him, splendorous festivals in commemoration of him, etc.. To all this he attached no little importance in his life, all this was so burdensome to him." Her advice on the matter was not heeded, and Krupskaya never publicly mentioned the mausoleum again and refused to visit it or stand atop it during celebrations. She also was offended by Petrograd's renaming as Leningrad, and she referred to the city in her correspondence as "Piter."[31]

Suprematist painter Kazimir Malevich had favored a cubical mausoleum, and he wanted the cube to serve as the symbol of the new Lenin cult. He hoped that each home in the country would have a replica of this cubical mausoleum, and viewed the cube as representative of everlasting life. He declared: "The cube is no longer a geometric body. It is a new object with which we try to portray eternity, to create a new set of circumstances, with which we can maintain Lenin's external life, defeating death."[32] Malevich saw art as a religion and as transcendent, and he believed that "revolutions in thought could be made through form." Form could help direct mankind to the promised land.[33]

Lenin's mausoleum is more pyramidal than cubical as it has become the "holy shrine" of communism and supports the Soviet leadership on its roof during the annual November 7 (anniversary of the Bolshevik revolution) and May 1 festivities. Children are often initiated into the Pioneer youth group there, high school graduates visit at the end of their studies, and newlyweds pay a call following their secular marriage ceremony. In 1941 soldiers departed from the mausoleum for the front, and a victory parade was staged before it in 1945. The first cosmonaut, Yuri Gagarin, appeared there both prior to and after his historic flight.[34]

In 1921, the Red Army began to organize "red corners" which featured expositions about Bolshevik leaders, including Lenin. Once he died, "Lenin corners" appeared at military facilities, schools, museums, factories and apartment buildings as the Lenin cult got underway; this form of exhibition was reminiscent of saints' corners which presented items associated with these hallowed individuals. Displayed pictures of Lenin were highly stylized in terms of expression, pose and gesture as in saintly icons.[35]

Stalin contributed to the Lenin cult just two days after the latter's demise when he started to collect memorabilia for delivery to the Lenin Institute. A newspaper in Minsk even tried, unsuccessfully, to have Sunday ("voskresenie") renamed "Leninden."[36] Lenin was similar to Jesus in that religious veneration was enhanced upon death, as were attributes of infallibility and ultimate truth. However, the Lenin cult included no mystification regarding his birth or his mother and Lenin lived to become the first pope of Soviet communism. He is buried astride the Kremlin, whereas the grave of St. Peter (rather than Jesus) rests, according to Catholic tradition, beneath the Vatican basilica.

Notes

1. For an interpretation of Lenin as a messiah, see Arnold Toynbee, *A Study of History*, abridgement of volumes I-VI (New York: Oxford University Press, 1946), p. 204.
2. Rene Fueloep-Miller, *The Mind and Face of Bolshevism* (New York: Harper and Row, 1965), p. 29.
3. Anatoly Lunacharsky, *Revolutionary Silhouettes* (London: Penguin Press, 1967), p. 40.
4. Nina Tumarkin, *Lenin Lives!: The Lenin Cult in Soviet Russia* (Cambridge: Harvard University Press, 1983), pp. 82-85.
5. Roy Medvedev, *Let History Judge* (New York: Knopf, 1971), pp. 149-50.
6. Tumarkin, pp. 119-20 and 132.
7. Tumarkin, pp. 126-27.
8. Tumarkin, pp. 139, 164 and 176. Walter Duranty, who covered Lenin's funeral for *The New York Times*, discerned a religious context but his account is somewhat hyperbolic: "What is happening here emphasizes the religious aspect of Bolshevism with Lenin as the central figure. How else can one explain the gigantic new movement to see his body - a movement not of Communists and their sympathizers alone, but of the rest of the population, despite such agony of cold?" See Walter Duranty, *I Write as I Please* (New York: Halcyon House, 1935), p. 223.
9. Tumarkin, p. 155. For an interpretation that Stalin may have outmaneuvered Lenin's widow Krupskaya, who had herself intended to deliver a eulogy, see Robert McNeal, "Krupskaia: The Feminine Subcult," in Bernard Eissenstat, ed., *Lenin and Leninism* (Lexington: Lexington, 1971), p. 221.
10. Tumarkin, p. 200.
11. Bertram Wolfe, *The Bridge and the Abyss* (New York: Praeger, 1967), p. 156.
12. Louis Fischer, *The Life of Lenin* (New York: Harper and Row, 1964), p. 674 and Isaac Deutscher, *Stalin: A Political Biography* (New York: Oxford University Press, 1961), p. 269.
13. Gaston Fessard, "Is Marx's Thought Relevant to the Christian?: A Catholic View," in Nicholas Lobkowicz, ed., *Marx and the Western World* (Notre Dame: University of Notre Dame Press, 1967), p. 366.
14. Tumarkin, pp. 229-31 and Fueloep-Miller, p. 217.
15. Brochure of January 21, 1925 reprinted in *Pravda*, January 21, 1990, p. 3.
16. Tumarkin, pp. 240-41.
17. Gregor Sebba, "Symbol and Myth in Modern Rationalistic Societies," in Thomas Altizer, William Beardslee and J. Harvey Young, eds., *Truth, Myth and Symbol* (Englewood Cliffs: Prentice-Hall, 1962), pp. 148-49. See also Boris Souvarine, *Stalin* (New York: Longmans, Green, 1939), p. 351.
18. Regis Debray, *Critique of Political Reason* (London: NLB, 1983), pp. 257-59.

19 Tumarkin, pp. 174-75. Historian Nicholas Vakar maintains that embalming Lenin was a form of idolatry appealing to the peasants. See *The Taproot of Soviet Society* (New York: Harper and Brothers, 1961), p. 88. Another historian, Robert McNeal, does not accept the report that Stalin opposed Lenin's cremation; such a plan to cremate would have been unlikely as there was no crematorium in Russia at that time. See *Stalin: Man and Ruler* (New York: New York University Press, 1988), p. 89.
20 Richard Stites, *Revolutionary Dreams* (New York: Oxford University Press, 1989), p. 120 and Tumarkin, pp. 176-78 and 181-84.
21 Robert McNeal, *Bride of the Revolution: Krupskaya and Lenin* (Ann Arbor: University of Michigan Press, 1972), p. 294.
22 Bernard Shaw, *The Rationalization of Russia* (Bloomington: Indiana University Press, 1964), p. 25. See also Peter Wiles, "On Physical Immortality," *Survey*, no. 56 (1965):128.
23 Tumarkin, p. 291n and Fueloep-Miller. p. 31.
24 Fischer, p. 675.
25 See Debray, p. 216 and Franz Borkenau, "The Concept of Death," *The Twentieth Century*, vol. 157 (April, 1955):313-29. During the Middle Ages, priors would tell monks during their induction ceremony that they would be granted eternal life in return for obedience. See Erik Erikson, *Young Man Luther (New York: W.W. Norton, 1958), p. 137.*
26 *The New York Times*, March 14, 1990. p. A4.
27 Peter Wiles, "On Physical Immortality," Part II, *Survey*, no. 57 (1965):142-61; Robert Williams, "Collective Immortality: The Syndicalist Origins of Proletarian Culture, 1905-1910," *Slavic Review*, vol. 39, no. 3 (September, 1980):392; George Kline, *Religious and Anti-Religious Thought in Russia* (Chicago: University of Chicago Press, 1968), pp. 164-65 and Glenn Tinder, "Eschatology and Politics," *The Review of Politics*, vol. 27 (July, 1965):324.
28 Mikhail Agursky, "Maksim Gorky and the Decline of Bolshevik Theomachy," in Nicolai Petro, ed., *Christianity and Russian Culture in Soviet Society* (Boulder: Westview, 1990), p. 79.
29 Mark Adams, "'Red Star': Another Look at Aleksandr Bogdanov," *Slavic Review*, vol 48, no. 1 (Spring, 1989):13-14 and *Pravda*, November 26, 1990, pp. 1 and 3.
30 Stites, p. 120; Tumarkin, pp. 201-204 and *Izvestiya*, April 19, 1988, p. 3.
31 McNeal, *Bride of the Revolution*, pp. 241-42.
32 Stites, p. 120 and Tumarkin, p. 190.
33 *The New York Times*, September 17, 1990, p. C13.
34 Christel Lane, *The Rites of Rulers* (Cambridge: Cambridge University Press, 1981), p. 210 and Fischer, p. 675.
35 Tumarkin, pp. 221-22 and 244.
36 Deutscher, p. 268 and Tumarkin, p. 233.

THE COMMUNIST RELIGION

Chapter VII

TENETS OF FAITH

Faith in communism developed during the nineteenth century and helped fill the void left by the decline of Christian influence during the Enlightenment.[1] Attraction was primarily psychological as many who had lost their Christian faith replaced it with a new belief system based on man's inherent "religious instinct." As explained by Douglas Hyde, a former British communist who became a Catholic, a lack of religious faith rather than poverty provided the impetus. He avers: "Communism is the child of unbelief. Bad social conditions are only the things on which it feeds."[2]

Communism is now in decline due to its own crisis of faith. Its goals have not been achieved, and force applied in Hungary and Czechoslovakia has led to an erosion of devotional support. As expressed by a Soviet journalist, man no longer understands himself or the world and he has not yet established new values to replace those that have been lost.[3] A new spiritual vacuum has thus been created into which competing faith systems will attempt to move.

The Essence of Belief

Longshoreman-philosopher Eric Hoffer maintains that truth within mass movements comes to be based on holy writ rather than experience or observation and that doctrines are to be believed, not understood. They are most effective when unintelligible, vague or unverifiable as "a doctrine that is understood is shorn of its strength."[4] His remarks are highly pertinent to communism, even though it is ostensibly grounded in reason rather than faith, and they are consonant with the interpretation of exiled Romanian political analyst Vladimir Tismaneanu who portrays intellectual attraction to Stalinism as an effort to replace broken ties to traditional religions. Tismaneanu writes: "Stalin's liturgical Marxism, with its rudimentary teleology, was arduously espoused by people who would have sworn otherwise that dialectical materialism was the opposite of any fanaticism."[5]

Polish philosopher Leszek Kolakowski declares that Marxism is based on faith pretending to be knowledge, and American historian and critic Max Eastman says of his acceptance of Marxism: "I need never again cry out: 'I wish I believed in the Son of God and his second coming.'"[6] Professor of religion A.J. Conyers sees communism as a faith which demands devotion and sacrifice, while former French communist and philosopher Roger Garaudy asserts: "At the genesis of all revolutionary action lies an act of faith: the certainty that the world can be transformed, that man has the power to create something new and that each of us is personally responsible for this transformation."[7]

Writer and former American communist Howard Fast describes the religious fervor within the party, which to its members becomes a "Temple of God," and Italian writer Ignazio Silone indicates that joining the party was a conversion; it also represented an act of completre dedication as he expected to be separated from his family and job.[8] French novelist, poet and critic Andre Gide did not join the communist party, but he depicts his strong attraction to it as follows: "My conversion is like a faith. My whole being is bent toward one single goal, all my thoughts - even involuntarily - lead me back to it. In the deplorable state of distress of the modern world, the plan of the Soviet Union seems to me to point to Salvation."[9]

Faith requires personal involvement, preparation for action, devotion to duty and self-denial; to a great extent, it also incorporates suffering. Gide provides an acute observation on this latter point when he cites his own wealth and lack of any manual labor experience as factors which increased his sense of suffering. He indicates that he felt injustices more than others because he had personally been favored in life.[10] Of course, intellectuals have difficulty in relying exclusively on faith as they inevitably develop some doubts. Ninian Smart avers that they counteract deep uncertainty by stressing certainty on the surface so dogma becomes an obligatory mechanism of faith systems.[11] Arthur Koestler sees them psychologically fortifying themselves against doubt by building two layers of defense to ward off neurosis. The outer defense may include censorship of conflicting ideas, while the inner defense is unconscious and based on rationalization.[12] Not all communists are true believers who can accommodate themselves to the changing party line, interpretive scholasticism and the turning of doctrine into dogma.[13] Some have faith in the party itself and pay little attention to its theoretical pronouncements; some are cynical ideologues or rationalizers who are personally involved in the manipulation of doctrine; while others are sheer opportunists who join communist parties in power as a means of professional and social advancement. The party does not have the same religious appeal for all its adherents, but this is equally true of Christianity and does not detract from an evaluation of communism within the context of faith systems.

Belonging

Communism attracts followers not just through faith, but also through its sense of community. People want to be part of a fellowship that seems to care for their welfare.[14] Their participation in a collective contributes to belief, especially when ritualistic phrases and songs are employed, and Polish writer Czeslaw Milosz observes that communists have learned from Catholics that "faith is more a matter of collective suggestion than of individual conviction."[15] Ignazio Silone also compares communism and religion in their application of a psychological mechanism which encourages individual members to identify with the collective, and former American communist Dorothy Goode relates that she responded to structural authority by first being a devout Christian and then becoming a devout communist.[16]

Communism imposes a discipline that provides a sense of organizational readiness to undertake a mission. It emphasizes action based upon conviction, and may be likened to religion in accentuating the need to bear witness for the faith. The movement embodies historical certainty, necessity and meaning and creates the image that all absolute truths may only be found within it.[17] Former communist Wolfgang Leonhard describes the righteousness pervading the Comintern school which he attended in the Soviet Union. When he was criticized for his views and behavior, he assumed that he must have done something wrong and agreed that these criticisms must have been justified. Only later did he realize that his interrogators had exaggerated his thoughts and actions, attributing to him political positions he had never held and political acts he had never committed.[18]

Mass movements impose a moral order and, as Eric Hoffer points out, they may operate without belief in God but not without belief in the Devil.[19] Communists feel that they are combatting oppression not just in their own country but, through alignment with other communist parties, throughout the world. They view their movement as incorrupt and willing to make sacrifices for the cause; as stated by former American communist Bella Dodd, communists see injustice anbd decadence outside their party but within it there is morality, order and certitude.[20] Participation in this moral community, and dedication to an ideal, contribute to a psychological predisposition to immortality as feelings about death are subordinated to projections of a perfect future society.[21]

Leaving a communist party can be traumatic. Defectors often need some emotional substitute for the party's doctrinal certainty and feeling of security, and they sometimes turn to an anti-communist totalitarianism. Fear of reentering the non-communist world can therefore trigger the defense mechanism which continues to portray it as inherently evil. Expulsion from a communist party may be even more searing as it has strong religious overtones related to excommunication and damnation of the soul.[22]

Ideology and Psychoreligion

The communist ideology of Marxism-Leninism bears many similarities to religion. Ideology has a millenial quality, and communist ideology may be viewed as a form of secular chiliasm incorporating a message of salvation.[23] Ideologies and religions are subsumed within classifications such as "worldviews" and "faith movements," and communist rule could be called an "ideocracy," a type of theocracy minus God.[24]

Ideology is like religion as its long-range perspective provides confidence that present calamities are just passing phenomena, and its combination of doctrine and praxis exudes a religious fervor as it furnishes a sense of direction. Both ideology and religion serve to motivate the masses, and are capable of reducing their tenets to simplified forms. Communism has been compared to Gnosticism, an early Christian school of thought stressing rationalism, and it has an underlying moral tone that led American communist Bella Dodd to remain faithful to Soviet goals for many years due to a "desire to see man-made perfection in this imperfect world." Political ideologies are often state-centered, but communism has a broader universal appeal that enhances its religious nature.[25]

Marxism-Leninism has replaced Christianity as the dominant value system in many societies, and it has a similar future orientation that influences contemporary reality. Its close functional relationship to Christianity has eased the transition to a pro-communist stance of religious Christians such as Andre Gide and the British poet and literary critic Stephen Spender; indeed Richard Crossman, a British journalist and politician who has studied the attraction of intellectuals to communism, cites a "Christian conscience" as an important factor. The symbiotic connection between communism and Christianity is also illustrated by a 1953 poll of voters for the Communist Party of Italy who were not themselves party members: 67 percent professed a belief in God, 76 percent said that one may simultaneously be a good communist and a good Catholic, and 78 percent identified themselves as Christians despite voting for an atheistic party.[26]

In a Marxist sense, psychoanalysis is like religion as both are ideologies that mask reality. They delve into man's essence, finding a basic fear of death. Psychoanalytical terms such as rationalization, substitution, transference, displacement and sublimation are all explainable within the context of ideology, thereby making psychoanalysis an analytic tool useful in the study of Marxist belief systems.[27]

Psychiatrist Thomas Szasz argues that psychiatry and religion are both "healing arts" that resemble communist practices. Psychiatry classifies people as mentally ill in order to stigmatize them socially and to create scapegoats who may be persecuted; the Soviet system often resorted to scapegoatism by claiming the existence of "class enemies" or "capitalist wreckers." So too is psychiatry used as a punishment, which is akin to the Soviet Union's detention of dissidents such as Yosif Brodsky and Valery Tarsis as mental deviants requiring therapy. To Szasz, mental health and illness have largely replaced the religious functions previously performed by God and the Devil. He sees psychiatric ideology as based on Christian theology, but man is born into sickness rather than sin and is guided by the doctor rather than the priest. Psychiatry, as had Christianity before it, identifies the presence of mental illness - the Devil - and uses this power as a means of social control.[28] Andre Gide presents an account of his visit to the Soviet town of Bolshevo, where all inhabitants were reformed criminals. To him, it represented the redemptive capacity of communism, but it may also be interpreted as an example of effective social control. Gide writes: "It leads one to think that all crimes are imputable not to the man himself who commits them, but to the society which drives him to commit them. One of these men, then another were invited to speak, to confess their former crimes, to relate how they had been converted, how they had come to recognize the excellence of the new regime and the personal satisfaction they experienced in submitting to it."[29]

Communism is a form of religion which helps man achieve salvation; it is a form of psychoanalysis which helps man overcome deviance; and it is a form of ideology which helps man discern and combat the contradictions inherent in his civilization.

Political Ideology

Members of non-governing communist parties are likely to be true believers, but members of ruling parties may be seekers of power concerned with status, perquisites and economic advantage. Communism parallels the fourth century institutionalization of Christianity in Rome as the ascent of a faith movement to political office comes to blend doctrine with patriotism and produces many loyal subjects who, in a religious sense, are content to go through the motions of observance. Stalin said that anything furthering Soviet power contributed toward the achievement of world communism, a credo that weakened Marxism's moral underpinning but solidified Soviet state legitimacy. Ideology may have been reduced to the pragmatism of realpolitik, but it nevertheless set standards of conformity within Soviet society and supplied a frame of reference, even for non-believers.[30] Soviet citizens tended to describe political events in terms of economic causality, and they responded to the question "who are you?" with the answers "worker" or "peasant."

In addition to serving as a source of regime legitimacy and contextual interpretation, political ideology pervades the socialization process through which citizens acquire their values and helps mobilize the populace against perceived ideological foes such as capitalists or imperialists. It also provides group cohesion for party members (as for any church) through study of unifying doctrinal positions and utilization of a common technical jargon. Communists and Catholics are similar in this regard.

Some communist leaders may not have actually believed their own Marxist-Leninist ideology, but they used it as an instrument to influence and control the masses. It became a technique of rule exercized by politicians who were well aware of their own resort to manipulation. They could smugly argue that proletarians lacked appropriate "political consciousness" and needed guidance from a party vanguard, and that "proletarian internationalism" was anything that benefited the interests of the Soviet Union. In reality, they probably recognized that the party bureaucracy dominated the working class and that the world's communist parties were, until recently, subordinating their own concerns to Soviet dictate.[31] It is to the masses, however, that such ideological gymnastics were directed. Wolfgang Leonhard explains how they were prevalent when he was a student in the Soviet Union as subjects were treated differently depending on the ideological context. He was told that dilapidated housing in the West was due to the impoverishment of the working class, but similar housing in the Soviet Union was a relic from the pre-revolutionary past.[32]

Political ideologies are "mobilized belief systems" which require aktivs to disseminate their values, and an authority structure to orchestrate them. When Gorbachev came to power in the Soviet Union in 1985, there were eleven million party aktivs and coordination was accomplished by the Central Committee's Department of Agitation and Propaganda. Marxism-Leninism becomes so embedded in the society's norms that it acquires its own historical dynamic irrespective of the elite's possible cynicism.[33] Historian Nicholas Vakar describes it as an "incantation in the ceremonies of headship" used to sanctify actions, and he compares the official jargon to stereotyped Church Slavonic homilies and prayers. It is a dead langauage unspoken by the people, but voiced by authority.[34] Nevertheless, its values are pervasive. Douglas Hyde relates how his woek as a journalist was affected by ideology even after he had become somewhat disillusioned with communism: "Marxist analysis was becoming a science to me without being an apostolic faith. I could use my Marxist methodology coldly for the larger part of the time, with the result that I was doing it more successfully than before."[35]

Communism is a faith system, despite evident elite manipulation of its doctrines and praxis, as its ideal is not obliviated by its methods. A classless society in which each receives according to his needs is still a spiritual vision even if a communist party dictatorship is not the means most conducive to its realization. So too has the passage of two millenia failed to bring to fruition Christianity's vision of the Kingdom of God.[36]

Faith systems come to emphasize organizational cohesion, which can be undermined by any doctrinal laxity. Their internal unity is constantly threatened by heresy and schism, but their institutional authority remains basically intact and continues to serve as a unifying force leading toward a potential ideal. In this regard, Christianity is likely to outlive communism as its goal is not quite earthly and its achievements are not measurable in concrete political and economic terms.

Notes

1. See Arthur Koestler, *The Yogi and the Commissar* (New York: Macmillan, 1945), pp. 112-14.
2. Douglas Hyde, *I Believed* (New York: G.P. Putnam's Sons, 1950), p. 299.
3. Elgiz Pozdnyakov, "The End of History?," *New Times*, no. 2 (January 9-15, 1990):33.
4. Eric Hoffer, *The True Believer* (New York: Harper and Row, 1951), pp. 78-79.
5. Vladimir Tismaneanu, *The Crisis of Marxist Ideology in Eastern Europe: The Poverty of Utopia* (London: Routledge, 1988), p. 64.
6. George Urban, ed., *Stalinism* (New York: St. Martin's, 1982), p. 277 and Daniel Aaron, *Writers on the Left: Episodes in American Literary Communism* (New York: Harcourt, Brace and World, 1961), p. 32.
7. A.J. Conyers, "Communism's Collapse: The Receding Shadow of Transcendence," *Christian Century*, vol. 107, no. 15 (May 2, 1990):466 and Roger Garaudy, *The Alternative Future* (New York: Simon and Schuster, 1974), p. 83.
8. Howard Fast, *The Naked God* (London: Bodley Head, 1958), p. 60 and Richard Crossman, ed., *The God That Failed* (New York: Bantam, 1954), p. 168.
9. Crossman, p. 173. Kenneth Murphy avers: "Gide, Koestler and Silone show us that communist intoxication was not the result of indifference to religious questions. On the contrary, it resulted from man's anguish at his inability to answer religious questions positively, which incites a feeling of cosmic hopelessness." See *Retreat From the Finland Station* (New York: The Free Press, 1992), p. 163.
10. Hoffer, p. 19; Hadley Cantrill, *The Politics of Despair* (New York: Basic Books, 1958), pp. 66-76 and Crossman, p. 168.
11. Ninian Smart, *Beyond Ideology* (San Francisco: Harper and Row, 1981), p. 301.
12. Koestler, pp. 118-19.
13. See Raymond Aron, *The Opium of the Intellectuals* (New York: W.W. Norton, 1957), pp. 276-77, 320 and 323 and Robert V. Daniels, *The Nature of Communism* (New York: Random House, 1962), p. 320.
14. See Daniels, p. 325 and Cantril, p. 86.
15. Czeslaw Milosz, *The Captive Mind* (New York: Vintage Books, 1951), pp. 189-90.
16. Crossman, p. 100 and Vivian Gornick, *The Romance of American Communism* (New York: Basic Books, 1977), p. 108.
17. See Whitakker Chambers, *Witness* (New York: Random House, 1952), pp. 9 and 26; Daniel Bell, *The End of Ideology* (Glencoe: Free Press, 1960), p. 371; Frank Meyer, *The Molding of Communists* (New York: Harcourt, Brace and World, 1961), p. 63 and Hoffer, p. 78.
18. Wolfgang Leonhard, *Child of the Revolution* (London: Ink Links, 1979), pp. 199-205.

19 Hoffer, p. 89.
20 See Harold Laski, *Reflections on the Revolution of Our Time* (New York: Viking Press, 1943), p. 72; Fast, p. 60 and Bella Dodd, *School of Darkness* (New York: Devin-Adair, 1954), p. 126.
21 John Marcus, *Heaven, Hell, and History* (New York: Macmillan, 1967), pp. xix-xxi and 182.
22 See Crossman, p. 226; Gabriel Almond, *The Appeals of Communism* (Princeton: Princeton University Press, 1954), p. 379; Dodd, p. 245 and Fast, pp. 60-61.
23 Reo Christenson, Alan Engel, Dan Jacobs, Mostafa Rejai and Herbert Waltzer, *Ideologies and Modern Politics* (New York: Dodd, Mead, 1971), p. 12 and Kurt Hutten, *Iron Curtain Christians* (Minneapolis: Augsburg, 1967), p. 474. For a discussion of religion as ideology, see John Plamenatz, *Ideology* (New York: Praeger, 1970), pp. 91-92.
24 See Ninian Smart, *Worldviews: Crosscultural Explorations of Human Beliefs* (New York: Charles Scribner's Sons, 1983), p. 2 and Daniels, p. 315. For an analysis of the Soviet system as an "ideocratic despotism," see Carl Linden, *The Soviet Party State: The Politics of Ideocratic Despotism* (New York: Praeger, 1983).
25 Zbigniew Brzezinski, *The Soviet Bloc*, revised and enlarged edition (Cambridge: Harvard University Press, 1967), pp. 489-90; Leon Baradat, *Political Ideologies: Their Origins and Impact*, third edition (Englewood Cliffs: Prentice-Hall, 1988), pp. 1-2; Alain Besancon, *The Rise of the Gulag* (New York: Continuum, 1981), p. 9; Dodd, p. 139 and David Apter, "Political Religion in the New Nations,," in Clifford Geertz, ed., *Old Societies and New States* (New York: Free Press, 1963), p. 92.
26 Chambers, p. 11; Crossman, p. 6 and Cantril, pp. 97-98.
27 David Apter, "Introduction: Ideology and Discontent," in David Apter, ed., *Ideology and Discontent* (New York: Free Press, 1964), p. 20; Ernest Becker, *Escape From Evil* (New York: Free Press, 1975), p. 163; Max Eastman, *Marxism: Is It Science* (New York: W.W. Norton, 1940), pp. 107-108 and Jules Monnerot, *Sociology and Psychology of Communism* (Boston: Beacon Press, 1960), p. 285.
28 Thomas Szasz, *Ideology and Insanity* (Garden City: Anchor Books, 1970), pp. 5-6, 21, 27, 29-30, 72, 76 and 239. On Soviet political scapegoatism, see Donald Barry and Carol Barner-Barry, *Contemporary Soviet Politics*, fourth edition (Englewood Cliffs: Prentice-Hall, 1991), pp. 5-6. Religions other than Christianity, such as Judaism, have also attempted to control their environments in an effort to prevent deviation.
29 Andre Gide, *Return From the U.S.S.R.* (New York: Knopf, 1937), pp. 89-90.
30 See Raymond Bauer, Alex Inkeles and Clyde Kluckholm, *How the Soviet System Works* (New York: Vintage, 1960), pp. 37-38. Milovan Djilas asserts that there are no longer any Marxists or Leninists in the Soviet Union and declares: "All these structural and ideological changes in the Soviet Union

have progressed from a way of thinking into merely a mode of expression." See "The Disintegration of Leninist Totalitarianism," in Irving Howe, ed., *1984 Revisited* (New York: Harper and Row, 1983), p. 140.

31 See Herbert Marcuse, *Soviet Marxism* (New York: Columbia University Press, 1958), p. 9; Erich Fromm, *Beyond the Chains of Illusion* (New York: Simon and Schuster, 1962), p. 147; George Orwell, *The Road to Wigan Pier* (London: Secker and Warburg, 1959), p. 178; Nicholas Vakar, *The Taproot of Soviet Society* (New York: Harper and Brothers, 1961), p. 129 and Leszek Kolakowski, *Main Currents of Marxism* (Oxford: Clarendon Press, 1978), pp. 465-67.

32 Leonhard, p. 27.

33 Mostafa Rejai, *Comparative Political Ideologies* (New York: St. Martin's, 1984), p. 9; Thomas Remington, *The Truth of Authority* (Pittsburgh: University of Pittsburgh Press, 1988), pp. 7 and 54 and Marcuse, p. 9.

34 Vakar, pp. 131-33.

35 Hyde, p. 212.

36 See the views of Andre Gide in Crossman, p. 196.

Chapter VIII

THE SPIRITUAL QUEST

Marxism has the attributes of a prophetic religion with messianic and apocalyptic traits. The institutionalization of a Russified version of Marxism in the Soviet Union has subordinated the vision of a classless society to the exigencies of bureaucratic and totalitarian rule, but communism nevertheless operates as a faith system in which a mass movement is motivated and controlled by a political ideology. Christianity may be defined as a faith system based on trust in God through Christ; communism as a faith system based on trust in the dialectic through the party. Christianity is classified as a religion, but does Soviet communism also qualify for this label?

What is Religion?

Religions are faith and action systems which help distinguish the sacred from the profane. The sacred is described through the language of myth and ritual, and it may include places, objects, traditions, principles, writings or persons.[1] It is reinforced through dogma enunciated by a leadership which in some religions is constituted as a clergy, and it is viewed as immutable and possibly based on divine revelation. A demonology helps identify the profane, and deviations from observance of the sacred could produce the charge of heresy and result in excommunication or banishment. Religions offer hope, salvation, consolation and fellowship, but demand in return duty and some degree of self-denial.[2]

Social scientist Robert Bellah defines religion as "a set of symbolic forms and acts that relate man to the ultimate conditions of his existence."[3] Functionally, it deals with issues such as the meaning of life, relations with others, coping with death and overcoming individual shortcomings as it seeks to explain the nature and causality of evil and suffering. It provides ethical guidance, an interpretation of order in the universe and a strong psychological underpinning that makes it personal in contrast with the greater abstraction of philosophy. Religion may explain the subordination of the ego to a broader awarenesss, and the dedication of an individual toward an end outside of oneself.[4]

Belief in God is not essential to religion. Psychoanalyst Erich Fromm maintains that religious experiences may be non-theistic, atheistic or even anti-theistic and it is evident that Confucianism and early Buddhism were not based on worship of any divinity.[5] Rather than a theology, religions require a teleology which delineates ends, sets forth a purpose and distinguishes final causes.

Is Communism a Religion?

Soviet communism is considered a group oriented religion by numerous social scientists, historians and theologians who see it as a salvation movement committed to deliverance from evil via a dialectical force impelling society toward an optimistic end. It aims at creating a moral order, and derives its teachings from sacred scripture.[6] Communism seeks to replace religions such as Christianity, and its virulent attacks on them have an underlying religiosity intolerant of competition. Its militant anti-theism not only denies the existence of God, but suppresses other movements to make sure that there must be no God. As interpreted by Catholic archbishop Fulton Sheen, this means that communists must realize that God exists; otherwise, they would be Don Quixotes dueling with imaginary windmills.[7]

Communism replaces God with man and creates a form of collective social idolatry based on authoritarian ethics. However, idolatry is itself religious and the communist focus on man represents a transcendental humanisn described in materialistic terms. As humanist philosophies came to substitute for religions during the Enlightenment, they assumed many of their attributes and functions even though they differed on the issue of divine moral sanction.[8] Communism incorporates the concept of the sacred, which extends beyond theistic religions and may be found in the progressive force of technology that moves the proletariat toward salvation.[9] Theologian Thomas Altizer writes that all religions provide a path from the sacred to the profane, and he avers: "Yet the sacred that becomes manifest through a negation of the profane must be a primordial Reality, an original paradise that has been hidden or lost by the advent of the profane, and thus a paradise that can be actualized by an unveiling or a reversal of the present."[10] Although he does not refer to communism, his remarks are acutely reminiscent of man's fall into class conflict and his redemption in a classless society.

Soviet communism is derived from Marxism, whose scientific credentials may tend to obfuscate its religiosity. Actually, science and religion are similar in their theoretical, experiential and transformative components and Marxism is more teleological than mechanistic. It therefore, like religion, is future oriented as the ultimate purpose is yet to be achieved; science is more past oriented as causes must be found to explain present events.[11]

Marxism, although in part a science based on historical materialism, is rooted in religious faith and is a myth system garbed in sociological and economic vestments.[12] The progression of man to the communist stage of development is as yet unproven, and Marx's denial of an antithesis to communism undermines his scientific claims. Religion permeates the Marxist outlook, and Regis Debray is on the mark when he claims that communists have commitment prior to intellectual rationalization and are attracted to the movement before they have read Marx and Lenin.[13] In the Soviet Union, the mythic and religious elements of Marxism are accentuated at the expense of the scientific elements. Rene Fueloep-Miller asserts that Bolshevism was registered in the "ikon corner" of Russian consciousness as its emphasis on technology and mechanism was received by the people as a form of religion. He writes: "Just as pious mystics once strove to make themselves into an image of God, and finally to become absorbed in Him, so now the modern ecstatics of rationalism labour to become like the machine and finally to be absorbed into bliss in a structure of driving belts, pistons, valves and fly-wheels."[14]

Soviet communism is both atheistic and anti-theistic but it bears, as observed by Berdyaev, the paradoxical message that God must be denied so that an earthly Kingdom of God may be established.[15] It is inherently religious as a belief system and, as will be demonstrated, is strongly religious in both function and form.

Bonding

Myths are an expression of the sacred which provides religions with dynamism as they link the past and future. They deal with collective aspirations, derive from the unconscious and are based on desires more than logic. Myths evolve out of the imagination, and lead man into transcendence. However, mythic thinkers may be unaware of the mythic qualities of their thoughts and may believe that they are reflecting upon an empirical reality.[16]

Myths often include action by God, or an assortment of gods, but they are also pertinent to Marxist systems in which the proletariat is assigned a mythical role of salvation and science is mythically presented as embedded in the dialectic.[17] As practiced in the Soviet Union, Marxism has exhibited totalitarian attributes and myths may thus have served the function of diverting the populace from harsh contemporary circumstances toward an eventual sacred reality. The promise of a utopian society operated as a legitimizing myth with the system attempting to demonstrate its immortality through an emphasis on youth and sports, and ceremonies performed before an eternal flame.[18]

In religions, ritual is the linkage between myth and the believer. It is the broader ceremonial structure of a community, whereas the term rite applies to more specific ceremonial practices. Ritual is a means of stressing the sacred and may be used politically to legitimize the ruling system. It may be directed by an elite with the aim of fostering group cohesion and conformity, and its role is largely psychological as it imbues events with a transcendent symbolism.[19] The most holy rites performed are deemed sacraments, which in the Soviet case may include pilgrimages to Lenin's tomb or speeches made from atop it on revolutionary anniversaries. Another rite with religious implications is the distribution of red handkerchiefs to each child initiated into the Pioneers youth group; the children are told that the handkerchief is a "sacred talisman" that represents the blood of revolutionary martyrs.[20]

The Way

Communism operates on the basis of an absolute truth which is known to those in authority. Lenin's depiction of a party vanguard possessed of political consciousness echoes the majoritarian certitude of

Rousseau's "general will" as it justifies the elitism of hierarchical control. The laws of history, as revealed in the sacred writings of Marx and Lenin, are indisputable as any challenge to their validity is labeled morally repugnant and evolutionally obstructive. Exclusivity regarding the truth obviates the right or need to test it as the party's guiding role over the masses is sanctified.[21] The party becomes infallible logically as it represents the "active principle in History," the proletariat, and infallible morally as its aims are in accord with the dialectic.[22]

Communism shares much with Catholicism in this regard. In the eleventh century, Pope Gregory VII declared that the Church of Rome had never erred and would never err, and that his own decisions were absolute; in 1885, Pope Leo XIII indicated that equal tolerance of all religions was equivalent to atheism. So too did the Communist Party of the Soviet Union acquire these characteristics; an October 1931 article by Stalin, according the status of infallibility to Lenin, paralleled the Vatican Council's proclamation in 1870 that the pope, at that time Pius IX, was infallible on all matters of faith and morals.[23]

Absolute truth engenders dogma, which is divinely revealed and immutable, and doctrine, which is also considered to be the word of God but is the basis of religious teaching rather than ecclesiastical affirmation. Dogma leaves out facts not consistent with it and presents a fixed perspective (although debates as to its content do take place within the clergy) which attempts to objectify ideas based on faith. It rejects intellectual relativizing as its truth supersedes changing analyses of history and, in a sense, presents man with the truth in order to free him from being a prisoner of history. Accepting dogma indicates man's submission to God and recognition that God's truth may be beyond human reason.[24]

For communists faith in the dialectic replaces faith in God, and the party substitutes for the Christian clergy.[25] As described by political scientist Gabriel Almond, the postulates of communism and Christianity have similar functions and they are interpreted by an apostolic succession, which for the communists includes Marx, Engels and Lenin.[26] A close-minded "mercenary consciousness" is produced which treats dissent as morally anomalous or treasonous. Soviet foreign minister Vyacheslav Molotov best exemplified this "mercenary consciousness" as he continued to affirm his acceptance of party dogmas even as his wife was being falsely castigated as an "enemy of the people" and sent into exile in Kazakhstan.[27]

Absolute truth leads to a process of demonization which vilifies supposed enemies of this truth and calls for their eradication. Mass movements tend to have a belief in some form of evil antagonist, a trait evident in fourteenth and fifteenth century Catholicism and the Stalinist Soviet Union. Whereas Catholics saw the devil operating in daily life, communists have identified a wide panoply of adversaries including imperialists, the ancien regime, clerical reaction, right wing social democrats, Trotskyites, kulaks, wreckers and cosmopolitans.[28]

Within the community of believers, the most serious dangers are schism and heresy. Schism is a split within a movement due to contested legal authority, but it is heresy which challenges absolute authority as it is the product of dogmatic and doctrinal divergence and also challenges the interpretative power of the clergy. The heretic is more menacing than the apostate who leaves a church as he claims to follow tradition and accuses the leadership of deviation. To church authorities, heresy is equivalent to state treason and the heretic is viewed as more offensive than the non-believer as he distorts the absolute truth and offends God. A pagan may be converted, but a heretic often ends up at the stake. Unlike a sinner who may have erred, the heretic is considered evil.[29] Communist sinners may engage in self-criticism and remain within the fold, as happened with Molotov in 1956 when he mistakenly declared that the Soviet Union was building socialism, but communist heretics are banished or killed, witness the exiling of Trotsky and his subsequent assassination.

Sinners are purified through penance. Richard Wright describes the internal trial of an American communist who was accused of harboring incorrect political views. Rather than call upon any witnesses to defend himself against the charges, he admitted guilt on all counts. As Wright relates: "Ross had not been doped; he had been awakened. It was not a fear of the Communist Party that had made him confess, but a fear of the punishment that he would exact of himself that made him tell of his wrongdoings. The communists had talked to him until they had given him new eyes with which to see his own crime."[30]

Within the religion of communism, the party is dedicated to the mission of propagating its beliefs; members join for life. Its authority is based more on a future vision than a present reality, and it claims possession of an ultimate truth which can only be found within its own corpus. Objectivity is defined as always putting the party first, whereas the sin of subjectivity is placing something ahead of the party.[31]

As the party embodies the truth, it monopolizes education and the dissemination of facts. The dictatorship of the proletariat becomes an ideological theocracy dominated by the intelligentsia as codified rules of conduct and technical jargon are controlled by full-time functionaries:

the apparat or clergy. Like theologians and canon lawyers, they bear the key to the deciphering of communications and thereby gain access to the sacred. Communist jargon is basically unintelligible to the masses (although they do glean knowledge from the media at a different level) and its role is thus comparable to Latin, Geez or Sanskrit.[32]

Reflections

Although communism qualifies as a religion in many ways, evident differences also exist. There is no concept of the supernatural or revelation, and the holy books are considered scientific rather than divinely inspired; the dialectic therefore serves as a substitute for God. Salvation (as in Judaism) is collective rather than individual and, in contrast to Christianity, there is no afterlife or practice of the virtues of humility and love. There is additionally no real worship based on prayer, although some form of liturgy is operative and hymns are sung.[33] Fasting is not utilized as a means of self-purification or as an aid to contemplation, and there is no formalized system of sainthood as in Catholicism even though Lenin may be considered canonized. Communism's materialism need not be seen as an impediment to religious interpretation since the Greeks and Romans had numerous gods who represented material things.

Whether or not Soviet communism has an ethical basis is a subject engendering considerable controversy as ethics are concerned with the value rather than the causality of human conduct and are fundamental to religion. On the one hand, the ideal communist society is made possible by man's basic goodness and is expected to have a strong ethical foundation. Man prepares for this secular Kingdom of God by undergoing internal spiritual change, and the values deemed essential for this emerging "new Soviet man" are delineated in the moral code included within the 1961 Party Program. As technology powers societal change, man develops a new consciousness in preparation for a moral order devoid of class contradictions and alienation.[34]

On the other hand, the dialectic could be viewed as determinist, thus denying man's free will to make ethical choices. Leninist emphasis on tactics and means also undercuts Soviet morality, as does the somewhat artificial creation of a "new Soviet man" through totalitarian methods of political socialization.[35] The relativism evident in Soviet ethical considerations is also problematic as moral ideas lack any independent status; concepts of justice or right are thus dependent on class and societal analysis.[36] The means used by Soviet communists may therefore be ethically deficient but the envisioned ends, probably unrealizable, are firmly ethical in constitution. Actually, the concept of a "new Soviet man" conditioned by social controls paralleled the Jewish and Christian belief in internal change ("And I will give them a new heart, and put a new spirit within them." - Ezekiel, ll:19) which, in Biblical accounts, was divinely inspired.

Secular Religion and Revolutionary Transformation

Communism bears many attributes of theological religions but its concerns are earthly and closely related, especially in the Soviet case, to the exigencies of secular state authority. During the Enlightenment, politics was elevated to the status of religion as it institutionalized power which had for long been under ecclesiastical control. The secular was made sacred, a process eased by the separation of church and state which led the latter to assume many characteristics of a church. Scientific investigations discredited literal interpretations of many Biblical accounts and politics stepped into the breach to assert a new form of absolutism based on faith.[37] Thus "secular religion" was born, although the term was not coined until 1944 by the French political sociologist Raymond Aron.[38]

The Enlightenment brought forth Rousseau's "general will," a concept which provided a rationale for "forcing" people to be "free," and totalitarianism later arose based upon eschatological assumptions subordinating the means to the end. It was a "secular religion," and Soviet communism developed as one of its denominations.[39] Nazism did not qualify as a "secular religion" to the same degree as it was not completely atheistic and its rites incorporated Christian practices.[40]

Regis Debray observes that revolutions begin as festivals and end as ceremonies.[41] In the United States, a so-called "civil religion" is the result as religious and political symbolism mesh despite the constitutional separation of church and state. However, this "civil religion" differs from "secular religion" due to its lack of conflict with established churches and its highly Christian essence.[42] In France, the revolution of 1789 had powerful anti-Christian undercurrents and produced the most clearcut example of "secular religion" prior to the triumph of Bolshevism in 1917.

The French revolutionaries severely restricted the authority of their country's Catholic Church, Western Europe's wealthiest and most intellectually prominent, as they established a form of "secular religion" which soon developed overtones of God-building. Divorce was legalized; birth control made more readily available; civil weddings, baptisms and burials were instituted; and the church and state were officially separated. At the same time, numerous churches and monasteries were closed and hundreds of clerics were executed.

To replace Catholicism, the revolution itself evolved into a "secular religion" with Bastille Day serving as the dawn of the new age in which post-revolutionary man replaced the evil ancien regime.[43] Revolutionary songs were substituted for church hymns, a new civil calendar took the place of one previously imposed by the Church, and several state festivals were established including the Festival of the Unity and Indivisibility of the Republic. All churches in Paris, including Notre Dame, were turned into Temples of Reason and the Bishop of Paris was forced to resign. Elsewhere in France churches were converted, but on a lesser scale. Within these Temples of Reason, representations of saints were replaced by those of revolutionary martyrs as Marat, Lepelletier and Chalier became the symbolic focus of a new secular Trinity.[44]

The Jacobin clubs placed man at the center of their "secular religion," but their practices were clearly influenced by Christianity in terms of rites and vocabulary; a day in the new revolutionary calendar, decadi, was even reserved for sermons.[45] The Jacobins resembled the later Bolsheviks as members were subjected to criticism at public meetings and supplied confessions. Proceeding from the assumption that man is good, the Jacobins established the basis for totalitarianism, which to historian John Marcus is "the final price of secularizing the eschatology of salvation and the transcendent ideal."[46]

Out of this budding totalitarian secularism emerged the Jacobin leader Maximilien Robespierre, who imposed his deism upon the state religion by proclaiming the existence of a Supreme Being and instituting a Festival of the Supreme Being. Robespierre's efforts were later echoed by the Russian "God-builders," but they differed due to an underlying rejection of atheism.[47] Catholicism was replaced by a religion worshiping a God of Reason, and the soul was still held to be immortal. This humanist church was closely identified with the state as religious and national holidays were merged.

In 1795, churches were returned to Christian control; in 1804, Pope Pius VII attended the coronation of Napoleon; and, in 1806, the Christian calendar was reintroduced. Nevertheless, the French revolution engendered a strong tradition of secularism which produced Theophilanthropy, a form of ethical culture, and the positivist Auguste Comte's new religion which deified man and advocated a non-Christian calendar. In addition, the Comte de Saint-Simon rejected the Christian concept of the fall and envisioned an earthly paradise based on man's goodness. After his death, a secular church expounding his ideas was founded; it included rites for baptism, marriage and burial.[48]

Secularization, set in motion by the Enlightenment, was given added impetus by the French revolution. Rather than just countering Church authority and transferring previously religious functions to the secular sphere, it also filled the void left by the Church's narrowing role by establishing new forms of ritual that constituted "secular religion." Eventually, the Bolsheviks reinvigorated this revolutionary tradition as Moscow became the center of the communist religion, a secular Third Rome.

Notes

1. William Paden *Religious Worlds* (Boston: Beacon Press, 1988), pp. 11 and 49 and Winston King, *Introduction to Religion* (New York: Harper and Row, 1954), pp. 36-38.
2. Ninian Smart has classified what he views as religion's six dimensions: doctrinal, mythic, ethical, ritual, experiential and social. See *Worldviews: Crosscultural Explorations of Human Beliefs* (New York: Charles Scribner's Sons, 1984), pp. 7-8.
3. Robert Bellah, *Beyond Belief* (New York: Harper and Row, 1970), p. 21.
4. King, p. 451; C. Daniel Batson and W. Larry Ventis, *The Religious Experience* (New York: Oxford University Press, 1982), pp. 7-8 and 10; Crane Brinton, *Ideas and Men: The Story of Western Thought*, second edition (Englewood Cliffs: Prentice-Hall, 1963), p. 373 and Erich Fromm, *You Shall Be As Gods* (New York: Holt, Rinehart and Winston, 1966), pp. 58-60.
5. Fromm, p. 57.
6. King, p. 497; Alfred Meyer, *Leninism* (New York: Praeger, 1957), p. 286; John Bennett, *Christianity and Communism Today* (New York: Association Press, 1966), p. 45; Charles West, *Communism and the Theologians* (New York: Macmillan, 1958), p. 132; Reinhold Niebuhr, "The Religion of Communism," *Atlantic Monthly*, vol. CXLVII (April 1931):462, 465 and 469; Hewlett Johnson, *The Soviet Power* (New York: International Publishers, 1940), p. 314; Reinhold Niebuhr, "Christian Politics and Communist Religion," in John Lewis, Karl Polanyi and Donald Kitchin, eds., *Christianity and the Social Revolution* (New York: Charles Scribner's Sons, 1936), p. 442 and Will Herberg, *Faith Enacted as History* (Philadelphia: Westminster Press, 1976), p. 180.
7. Rene Fueloep-Miller, *The Mind and Face of Bolshevism* (New York: Harper and Row, 1965), p. 72; Nicolas Berdyaev, *The Russian Revolution* (Ann Arbor: University of Michigan Press, 1966), p. 84; Nicolas Berdyaev, *The Origin of Russian Communism* (Ann Arbor: University of Michigan Press, 1960), p. 158; Kurt Hutten, *Iron Curtain Christians* (Minneapolis: Augsburg, 1967), p. 468 and Fulton Sheen, *Communism and the Conscience of the West* (Indianapolis: Bobbs-Merrill, 1948), p. 168. Protestant theologian Paul Tillich discerns an underlying affirmation of God even when God is being denied as ultimacy is the prime concern. See *Dynamics of Faith* (New York: Harper and Row, 1956), pp. 45-46.
8. Berdyaev, *The Russian Revolution*, p. 79; Bennett, p. 82; Fromm, p. 56; Jacques Maritain, *True Humanism*, sixth edition (London: Geoffrey Bles, 1954), p. xiv and King, p. 496.
9. Paden, p. 167; Jacques Ellul, *The New Demons* (New York: Seabury Press, 1975), p. 73 and Jules Monnerot, *Sociology and Psychology of Communism* (Boston: Beacon Press, 1960), pp. 144-45.
10. Thomas Altizer, "The Sacred and the Profane: A Dialectical Understanding of Christianity," in Thomas Altizer and William Hamilton, *Radical Theology and the Death of God* (Indianapolis: Bobbs-Merrill, 1966), p. 141.

11 Teleological and scientific components may coexist. See Harold Schilling, *Science and Religion* (New York: Charles Scribner's Sons, 1962), p. 75 and W.T. Stace, *Religion and the Modern Mind* (Philadelphia: Lippincott, 1952), pp. 20-21.
12 Ellul, p. 184 and Ninian Smart, *In Search of Christianity* (San Francisco: Harper and Row, 1979), p. 309.
13 Regis Debray, *Critique of Political Reason* (London: NLB, 1983), p. 119.
14 Fueloep-Miller, p. 24. See also Berdyaev, *The Russian Revolution*, p. 58.
15 Berdyaev, *The Russian Revolution*, p. 26.
16 Ellul, pp. 120-21; Herberg, pp. 143-44 and 189; Roger Garaudy, *From Anathema to Dialogue* (New York: Herder and Herder, 1966), p. 41; Monnerot, p. 152 and Robert C. Tucker, *Philosophy and Myth in Karl Marx* (New York: Cambridge University Press, 1965), p. 224.
17 Robert Scranton, "Myth in Myth," in Thomas Altizer, William Beardslee and J. Harvey Young, eds., *Truth, Myth and Symbol* (Englewood Cliffs: Prentice-Hall, 1962), p. 84; Berdyaev, *The Russian Revolution*, p. 68 and Ellul, p. 103.
18 Thomas Altizer, "The Religious Meaning of Myth and Symbol," in Altizer, Beardslee and Young, pp. 93-94 and Lars Erik Blomqvist, "Some Utopian Elements in Stalinist Art," *Russian History*, vol. ll, nos. 2-3 (Summer-Fall, 1984):298-99.
19 Harold Fallding, *The Sociology of Religion* (Toronto: McGraw-Hill Ryerson, 1974), p. 81; Christel Lane, *The Rites of Rulers* (Cambridge: Cambridge University Press, 1981), pp. ll, 45 and 51; Michael Baigent, Richard Leigh and Henry Lincoln, *The Messianic Legacy* (New York: Henry Holt, 1986), p. 133 and Nicholas Vakar, *The Taproot of Soviet Society* (New York: Harper and Brothers, 1961), p. 116.
20 Baigent, Leigh and Lincoln, p. 133.
21 Harold Laski, *Reflections on the Revolution of Our Time* (New York: Viking, 1943), p. 73; Robert V. Daniels, *The Nature of Communism* (New York: Random House, 1962), p. 349; Frank Meyer, *The Molding of Communists* (New York: Harcourt, Brace and World, 1961), p. 23 and D.M. Mackinnon, "Christian and Marxist Dialectic," in D.M. Mackinnon, *Christian Faith and Communist Faith* (London: Macmillan, 1953), p. 229.
22 Arthur Koestler in Richard Crossman, ed., *The God That Failed* (New York: Bantam, 1954), p. 33.
23 Robert C. Tucker, "The Rise of Stalin's Personality Cult," *The American Historical Review*, vol. 84, no. 2 (April, 1979):356; Friedrich Gontard, *The Chair of Peter* (New York: Holt, Rinehart and Winston, 1964), p. 235 and John O'Brien, *The Inquisition* (New York: Macmillan, 1973), p. l.
24 Niebuhr, "The Religion of Communism," pp. 463 and 467; Monnerot, p. 153 and James Hitchcock in John Delaney, ed., *Why Catholic?* (Garden City: Doubleday, 1979), pp. 76-78. For a differing perspective on dogma, see Erik Erikson, *Young Man Luther* (New York: W.W. Norton, 1958), pp. 140-41. He writes: "Dogma, given total power, reinstates what once was

The Spiritual Quest 91

to be warded off, and brings back ancient barbaric ambiguities as cold and overdefined legalisms so unconvincing that, where once faith reigned, the law must take over and be enforced by spiritual and political terror."

25 Leszek Kolakowski, *Main Currents of Marxism*, vol. III (Oxford: Clarendon Press, 1978), p. 523 and Raymond Aron, *The Opium of the Intellectuals* (New York: W.W. Norton, 1957), p. 284.
26 Gabriel Almond, *The Appeals of Communism* (Princeton: Princeton University Press, 1954), p. 35.
27 Alexander Pumpyansky, "Liberation From Nightmare," *New Times*, no. 1 (January 1-8, 1990):40.
28 Leszek Kolakowski in George Urban, ed., *Stalinism* (New York: St. Martin's, 1982), p. 260; Adam Ulam in Urban, p. 132; John Kosa, *Two Generations of Soviet Man* (Chapel Hill: University of North Carolina Press, 1962), p. 37 and Eric Hoffer, *The True Believer* (New York: Harper and Row, 1951), p. 89.
29 Dale Vree, *On Synthesizing Marxism and Christianity* (New York: John Wiley and Sons, 1976), p. 15; Ellul, p. 184 and Arthur Koestler, *Arrow in the Blue* (New York: Macmillan, 1952), p. 257.
30 Crossman, p. 158. A similar process within Christianity has been described by Erik Erikson. He explains that when Martin Luther was living in an Augustinian monastery, there were weekly joint confessions regarding transgressions against the group and violations of the monastery's rules. Each monk was required to point out the transgressions of others, which then led to self-criticisms. See Erikson, p. 33.
31 Daniels, pp. 331 and 333; Czeslaw Milosz, *The Captive Mind* (New York: Vintage, 1951), p. 198; Giulio Girardi, *Marxism and Christianity* (New York: Macmillan, 1968), pp. 198-99 and Meyer, pp. 153-54. Poet Osip Mandelstam has described the party as an "inverted church" based on the deification of man. See Nadezhda Mandelstam, *Hope Abandoned* (New York: Atheneum, 1974), p. 20.
32 A. Rossi, *A Communist Party in Action* (Hamden, Connecticut: Archon Books, 1970), p. 209; Almond, pp. 14-15; Eduard Heimann, *Reason and Faith in Modern Society* (Middletown, Connecticut: Wesleyan University Press, 1961), p. 171 and Leonardo Boff, *Church: Charism and Power* (New York: Crossroads, 1985), pp. 84-85. Georgy Shakhnazarov, an adviser to Gorbachev, has said that political commissars in the Soviet military are equivalent to chaplains in other armies. See *The New York Times*, July 6, 1990, p. A7.
33 Meyer, p. 17 and Ellul, p. 187.
34 Richard De George, *Soviet Ethics and Morality* (Ann Arbor: University of Michigan Press, 1969), p. 6 and Ernst Benz, *Evolution and Christian Hope* (Garden City: Doubleday, 1966), p. 137.
35 Max Eastman, *Reflections on the Failure of Socialism* (New York: Grosset and Dunlap, 1955), chapter 7; Richard Stites, *Revolutionary Dreams* (New York: Oxford University Press, 1989), p. 101; Zbigniew Brzezinski, *The*

Grand Failure (New York: Charles Scribner's Sons, 1989), p. 231; Meyer, p. 18 and Robert Conquest, *The Politics of Ideas in the U.S.S.R.* (New York: Praeger, 1967), pp. 13 and 15.
36 Meyer, p. 56
37 David Apter, "Political Religion in the New Nations," in Clifford Geertz, ed., *Old Societies and New States* (New York: Free Press, 1963), p. 73; Ellul, pp. 167 and 176; Daniel Bell, *The End of Ideology* (Glencoe: Free Press, 1960), p. 372 and D.G. Charlton, *Secular Religions in France, 1815-1870* (London: Oxford University Press, 1963), p. 14.
38 Aron, p. 265. Secular religion is non-theological, but it has been argued that Christianity is in part secular as God is manifested in the form of an historical person, Jesus. See David Martin, *The Religious and the Secular* (New York: Schocken, 1969), p. 25.
39 Waldemar Gurian, "Totalitarianism as Political Religion," in Carl Friedrich, ed., *Totalitarianism* (New York: Grosset and Dunlap, 1954), pp. 123 and 128; Tony Smith, *Thinking Like a Communist* (New York: W.W. Norton, 1987), p. 21; Waldemar Gurian, *Bolshevism* (Notre Dame: University of Notre Dame Press, 1952), p. 5; Glenn Vernon, *Sociology of Religion* (New York: McGraw-Hill, 1962), p. 57; Nina Tumarkin, *Lenin Lives! The Lenin Cult in Soviet Russia* (Cambridge: Harvard University Press, 1983), p. 2; Richard Lowenthal, "Beyond Totalitarianism?," in Irving Howe, ed., *1984 Revisited* (New York: Harper and Row, 1983), p. 264 and Leszek Kolakowski, "Communism as a Cultural Formation," *Survey*, vol. 29, no. 2 (Summer, 1985):147.
40 See Lane, pp. 272-73.
41 Debray, p. 9.
42 Richard Fenn, *Toward a Theory of Secularization* (Norwich, Connecticut: Society for the Scientific Study of Religion, 1978), p. 41 and Lane, p. 256. For arguments that "civil religion" is not a religion, see Richard Neuhaus, "From Civil Religion to Public Philosophy," in Leroy Rouner, ed., *Civil Religion and Political Theology* (Notre Dame: University of Notre Dame Press, 1986), p. 102 and Richard Neuhaus, *Time Toward Home: The American Experiment as Revelation* (New York: Seabury Press, 1975), chapter 19.
43 Crane Brinton, *The Jacobins* (New York: Russell and Russell, 1961), p. 221.
44 See Albert Soboul, *The French Revolution, 1787-1799* (London: NLB, 1974), pp. 346-49 and Gontard, p. 483.
45 Brinton, *The Jacobins*, p. 205.
46 John Marcus, *Heaven, Hell, and History* (New York: Macmillan, 1967), p. 108.
47 See Carlton J.H. Hayes, *Nationalism: A Religion* (New York: Macmillan, 1960), p. 56.
48 Hayes, p. 56 and Charlton, pp. 68-69 and 88-89.

Chapter IX

THE SOCIAL GOSPEL

Communism and Christianity share basic ideas and similar evolutionary paths. Karl Marx, although ostensibly rejecting both Christianity and utopianism, was nevertheless influenced by Christian themes evident in nineteenth century utopian thought, and there is a long tradition of Christian visionaries who advance aspects of communalism. The Reformation gave rise to the works of Thomas More and Tommaso Campanella, while the Enlightenment produced the Comte de Saint-Simon's plea for a society based on a new Christianity distinct from either Protestantism or Catholicism. In America, the Amana Community and the Shakers represented a form of Christian communism ("He that hath two coats, let him impart to him that hath none." - Luke, 3:11); in England John Goodwyn Barmby tried to establish a communist church which secularized Christian rites, including baptism. Even the Old Believers in Russia, far removed from Enlightenment concepts, blended Christianity and communalism.[1]

The Double Helix

The path taken by Soviet communism in the twentieth century is reminiscent of Christianity's early evolution. Emphasizing communal values, Christianity appealed during its first three centuries after the death of Christ to the urban working class as its message was the salvation of the oppressed ("Blessed be ye poor: for yours is the Kingdom of God. Blessed are ye that hunger now: for ye shall be filled." - Luke, 6:20-21).[2]

Christianity gradually became Greco-Romanized, just as Marxism became Slavicized, and its social radicalism became submerged. Man's action, emphasized in the Jewish tradition, gave way to Hellenic concern with man's being just; historical self-realization was thus replaced by contemplation. In some ways, the concept of God changed from that of a worker to that of an aristocrat in a manner similar to Lenin's transition from Marxist proletarianism to a concentration on the intelligentsia serving as the vanguard.[3]

Christianity's shift of focus was the byproduct of its success as the strength of the Church became linked to the power of the Roman Empire. In the fourth century, Constantine adopted Christianity and authorized its practice within his realm; it was then made the state religion by Theodosius in 380. The Church took on the trappings of the Roman imperial structure as deference to authority took precedence over millenialism, sin was stressed rather than its possible elimination, and obedience took primacy over faith. An institutionalized Church developed as communalism and non-materialism ("Go to now, ye rich men, weep and howl for your miseries that shall come upon you." - James, 5:1) were superseded by hierarchy and inequality, with the Church itself becoming rich and accepting of the political order.[4] A clergy was established, which led to the naming of cardinals in the fifth century, a College of Cardinals in the twelfth century, and to enhanced papal authority culminating in eventual declarations of infallibility. Christianity drifted away from its Jewish traditions as it introduced the concept of celibacy, began to preserve the relics of saints, and granted indulgences for sin. Soviet communism experienced a parallel evolution as Lenin "Christianized" Marxism upon the Bolsheviks' assumption of power and ushered in communism as the new state religion. Ecclesiastical authority was asserted as the workers were subordinated to the party, the party became increasingly centralized rather than consensual, and economic inequality engendered advantages for the party's emerging "new class."

The absence of a Second Coming or the achievement of salvation through a Kingdom of God produced an institutionalized Church to set forth doctrine and retain the faith. St. Augustine, in his post-millenial ecclesiastical interpretation, did not expect an early advent of the Kingdom of God and he therefore stressed the need for extensive Church authority in the interim.[5] In like manner, Stalin said that communism's advent was far in the future; a powerful state had to be maintained. There was to be no withering; the state, in fact, had to be strengthened to withstand the challenge of class enemies.

The Christian dynamic of God working in history (derived from Judaism) was pushed aside by a new static vision of a hierarchical and institutional Church, a tendency reinforced when Aquinas incorporated Aristotelianism into Christianity. The schism of Catholic and Eastern churches in 1054 had already divided Christendom, but the Catholic Church had retained centralized control over its own universal flock in a form which liberation theologian Leonardo Boff labels "totalitarian." Boff also maintains that Jesus preached the Kingdom of God, not the Church; Czechoslovak philosopher Milan Machovec avers that Jesus' passivity toward authority was not aimed at accepting it but at encouraging man to change internally in preparation for the Kingdom of God.[6] The Church brought its own version of the Gospel to the masses and carefully controlled its interpretation. Laymen did not have access to the Bible, and those copies that were used by the clergy were in the publicly unfamiliar Latin rather than the vernacular. When Gutenberg first printed the Bible in 1455, the power of the clergy started to weaken. Increased accessibility of the Bible to the laity opened the way for doctrinal diversity, helping to generate the Reformation. In the communist world Khrushchev's endorsement of "different roads to socialism," and his initiation of an anti-Stalin campaign, had a similar impact; public discussion of doctrinal matters was stimulated and systems of national communism (in a manner common to Protestantism) started to evolve.

Christianity turned into a non-revolutionary movement supportive of the ruling class, just as Soviet communism became protective of the status quo and the interests of the dominating nomenklatura. So too did it distance itself from social problems and concerns about human rights. In this regard, political scientist Harold Laski asserted that the Christian "accepted personal slavery before the Reformation; and he accepted the slavery of the wage system after it."[7] In the Soviet Union communist rule also produced excessive abuses of human rights as, in both the Christian and Soviet cases, the theoretical ends were clearly subordinated to the means needed to cope with the realities of power. Also, in the area of economics, Christianity overlooked Jesus' admonitions regarding the accumulation of wealth ("Then said Jesus unto his disciples, Verily I say unto you, that a rich man shall hardly enter into the Kingdom of Heaven." - Matthew, 19:23) and accommodated itself to the rise of capitalism. Entrepreneurs were deemed eligible candidates for heaven, and spirituality was attributed to the labor performed by the working class. In communism, Khrushchev began to approve of some capitalist techniques; Gorbachev moved rapidly toward free enterprise and market economics despite the party's stated goals of eliminating both money and classes and distributing goods on the basis of need.

Christianity and communism had noble messages of salvation, but failure to achieve it led to claims that a source of structural authority, the Church or communist party, was required to find success in other ways: the Church would save the faithful and the communist party would build a socialist society. Once centralized and bureaucratic control was exercised, the means reduced the likelihood of realizing the end as politics came to supersede spiritual visions. There was no Second Coming or classless society, but each movement effectively built world churches committed to those goals.[8] The names of Jesus and Karl Marx continued to be invoked but, in the words of ethical philosopher Eugene Kamenka, their voices were not often heard.[9]

Images in a Mirror

Communism and Christianity are religions with linear views of history, messianic hopes and common goals of a non-materialistic peaceful society freed from alienation. For the communists, theoreticians substitute for theologians and dialectical materialism replaces faith in the Cross. Both religions share the theme of suffering, which engenders proletarian class consciousness or grace respectively. The world must be redeemed and made holy, revolutionary social change being required to eliminate iniquity ("But many that are first shall be last; and the last shall be first." - Matthew, 19:30). [10]

Communism and Christianity offer a sense of spiritual community or fellowship, and there is an historical purpose divorced from egotistic concern. Psychological communion provides refuge from anxieties, but those who violate group norms are expected to demonstrate contrition through confession and self-punishment.[11] Members join these movements for life and often signify their bonding by adopting new names, witness traditions regarding nuns and the revolutionary pseudonyms chosen by Ulyanov (Lenin), Djugashvili (Stalin) and Bronstein (Trotsky). It should be added, however, that hiding one's identity from the secret police was also a crucial factor in the Bolshevik case.

Family connections are subordinated to the movement, in part to prevent dynastic succession, but the forms are at variance as communists generally maintain a public silence about spouses and children (the U.S.

government did not know until his funeral that General Secretary Yuri Andropov had a wife) while Christianity developed a policy of celibacy for priests, monks and nuns. Soviet communism shares Christianity's underlying asceticism, a trait evident in Lenin's simple mode of life (he lived in a modest four-room apartment while serving as the Soviet leader), his punctuality and hard work, and his abstention from drinking or smoking.[12] Lenin also entered into a revolutionary marriage to Krupskaya that emphasized common ideological commitment more than the values of family.

Communism and Christianity share proselytizing tendencies aimed at spreading the gospel of ultimate salvation. Karl Marx belonged to the League of Communists, and then the International Workingmens' Association; Lenin established the Communist International in 1919. The Church constituted the Congregation for the Propagation of the Faith in 1622 to supervise the work of missionaries.[13]

Commissars and Cardinals

Communism has much in common with Catholicism in terms of organization and methods. Both have deviated from accentuating the communalism of workers and moved toward the authoritarianism of a structured church, yet they continue to select general secretaries and popes of humble class origin. Both have also become intellectually elitist, leading George Orwell to remark that for communists and Catholics "only the 'educated' are completely orthodox."[14] Since political success has been achieved, the distinction between spiritual and temporal authority has been obfuscated as popes have ruled over the Papal States, and now Vatican City; general secretaries of the Communist Party of the Soviet Union have moved into the state offices of prime minister and president.[15] This church-state symbiosis, symptomatic of theocracies, thus produces religious dogma, but political pragmatism. The Soviet Union set aside its ideological tenets for the sake of strategic expediency when entering into the Nazi-Soviet pact, just as the Church has reached accommodation with numerous repressive regimes (including Nazi Germany) in order to safeguard the faithful. It has argued that lay governments are only transitory, whereas the Church's mission is eternal.[16]

The structures of the Communist Party of the Soviet Union and the Roman Catholic Church are inherently authoritarian and pyramidal, based upon democratic centralism or guidance by the Holy Spirit.[17] Even strong critics of communism recognize such structural affinities, maintaining that similarities are actually exaggerations of Catholicism's most negative attributes or do not affect the perceived differences in content between the two religions.[18] Donald Smith, an expert on the interaction of religion and politics, compares authority in religious systems on the basis of three variables and concludes that Catholicism is highly authoritarian in all three dimensions and scores higher on his authoritarian value index than the other religions covered in his inquiry, namely Islam, Hinduism and Buddhism.[19] Such propensities within the Church are likely to appear structurally in the form of analogues to Marxist-Leninist practice.

Candidate members of the communist party are equivalent to novices entering a Catholic order, and the most able in each movement are selected for doctrinal training in orthodox schools. Communists are obligated to obey the party's rules, just as Catholics adhere to canon law and accept the guidance of the Corporal and Spiritual Works of Mercy. In essence, the party is like a clergy and its Central Committee may be compared to the College of Cardinals. In the Soviet Union, the Central Committee elects the general secretary and he in turn influences the selection of new Central Committee members and thereby controls his succession; at the Vatican, cardinals elect the pope and he chooses cardinals who participate in the selection of his heir to the throne of Peter. The Politburo and Curia are not directly parallel as the former has some control over the general secretary and is a policy-making body, whereas the latter has no formal authority over the pope but performs significant bureaucratic and administrative functions. In terms of worldwide movements, communism had its periodic congresses of the Communist International (Comintern) through 1935, but less formalized gatherings since then such as the Moscow party meetings of twelve parties in 1957 and of eighty-one parties in 1960. Catholicism still assembles bishops on an ad hoc basis for Ecumenical Councils; twenty-one have so far taken place. The Communist Party of the Soviet Union retains strong links to communist parties in other countries, as does the Church through its association with many Christian political parties.

Communism and Catholicism are closed systems in which political deliberations are far removed from public scrutiny. Candidates for high posts do not campaign and do not organize rival electoral slates, although evident change in this regard started to take place in the Soviet Union during the Gorbachev period.[20] General secretaries and popes are chosen in secrecy, and little information about the selection process is made publicly available afterward. In both systems, ethnicity has played a crucial role. The Politburo, until the 1990 reform, was dominated by Russians; all general secretaries except Stalin were also Russians. The Curia and the College of Cardinals have been heavily Italian, and most popes have also been Italian. Communists have often been compared to members of the Church's Jesuit order.[21] The Jesuits, founded by Ignatius Loyola as the Society of Jesus and formally established by Pope Paul III in 1540, played a major role in the Counter-Reformation when the Church needed activists to spread the faith rather than contemplative monastics. Jesuits passed through two years of candidacy as novices and were organized in a four-tier hierarchical structure. They renounced their own will and judgment and pledged obedience to their movement as a means of serving God.[22] Jesuits made frequent confessions and dedicated themselves completely to their cause at the expense of personal circumstances. They lacked local roots or a geographical base of operations, and gave up ties to relatives as they were assigned to missionary activity throughout the world. Their aim was to convert souls, with Francis Xavier's mission to Asia being comparable to that of Comintern agents during the twenties. The Jesuits, like the Bolsheviks, subordinated individualism to authority and stressed means as secondary to ends. Both highlighted activism and proselytization through the development of cadres, leading to similar structures of their movements.[23]

Scholasticism is a feature of communism and the Church. It evolved from the eighth through the fifteenth centuries as a means of reconciling faith and reason by applying philosophical concepts to the examination of doctrine, and reached its height in the thirteenth century when Thomas Aquinas incorporated Aristotelian logic into Christianity. In intent, Scholasticism was a methodology of philosophy rather than theology, but theologians often used it to buttress pre-conceived viewpoints and inquiry frequently was rooted in the affirmation of a proposition's conformity to revealed truths.[24] In this vulgarized sense, Scholasticism came to represent a rigid means of inquiry emphasizing intellectual arguments over minor details which attempts to demonstrate logically what is already believed religiously. Scholasticism is a "closed system" in which, according to Arthur Koestler, one proves what one believes and believes what one proves. "Closed systems" don't modify their beliefs, but erect "elastic defenses" to absorb the impact of new facts. Objective argumentation is eschewed as facts go through a "scholastic processing" which deprives them of value; any disagreement engenders the questioning of a speaker's psychological motivation.[25]

Soviet philosophy is rife with Scholasticism derived from communist religious assumptions, and party legitimacy is fostered (in a manner similar to that of the Church via its interpretations of Latin writings) by esoteric hermeneutic and exegetic analysis of arcane texts.[26] Marxism-Leninism and Thomism may indeed have more in common than any other two contemporary schools of thought as both reject phenomenalism and exhibit an epistemological realism derived from belief in an absolute truth.[27]

The communist party and the Vatican control their versions of the truth by monopolizing doctrinal development and imposing an orthodoxy of thought buttressed by censorship. General secretaries (until Gorbachev) and popes are never criticized in the media, and competing viewpoints are often condemned as heresies.[28] As the communists condemned Machism, Kautskyism and Trotskyism, so too did the Catholics vilify Montanism, Nestorianism, Pelagianism, Monophysitism and Jansenism. Until Gorbachev permitted some degree of "glasnost", Soviet publications were heavily censored; this parallels the Church's Index of Prohibited Books, instituted in 1559. Soviet purges are reminiscent of actions taken by the Holy Office of the Inquisition, renamed in 1965 as the Sacred Congregation for the Doctrine of the Faith.

Science often presents a threat to closed systems of thought due to its process of inquiry moving outside of religious tradition. Communists and clerics carry out scientific research, and even reconcile many scientific and religious principles, but conflict develops as science becomes increasingly specialized and delves into areas where religion is reluctant to tread. Eventually, science and religion have been able to be reconciled as the former has uncovered provable truths that could not be disregarded as fundamental to knowledge.[29]

In the Soviet Union, Marxism-Leninism is based on the supposed science of dialectical materialism, but pure scientific investigation has been hampered by rigid ideological controls. The late Stalinist period represented the peak of repression as the theories of ideologically approved biologists such as Lysenko and Michurin (who stressed environmental conditioning) had a chilling effect on free inquiry. Lysenko, in particular, deemed conformity with Marxism more important than experimental verification; he cited Marxist works rather than scientific ones, and questioned the class background of scientists.[30] Lysenkoism was not eliminated from Soviet science until the Brezhnev period.

Giordano Bruno was brought before the Inquisition in 1592 and convicted of heresy due to his philosophical views; he was burned alive in 1600. His ordeal was precipitated by his support for Copernican astronomical concepts, although he was not prosecuted on this basis as the works of Copernicus were not yet listed in the Index of Prohibited Books. The Church endorsed the Ptolemaic, earth-centered view of the universe and challenged Galileo's Copernicanism when he was called before the Inquisition in Rome in 1615. He too was accused of heresy but was given numerous warnings before being found guilty in 1633. The theories of Copernicus, which the Church had treated as hypotheses, became a cause of great concern once Galileo moved them into the category of alleged scientific truth; for the Church, Copernicanism was at variance with Scripture. The writings of Copernicus were thus placed on the Index, as were those of Galileo. In 1820, dissemination of the proposition that the earth revolved around the sun was finally permitted, and works on this subject were removed from the Index in 1835.[31]

Protestant Parallels

Communism is more often compared with Catholicism than Protestantism due to the centralized and institutionalized power of the Vatican and the concentration of authority in the hands of the pope. Protestantism is more variegated and fissiparous, and is frequently related to capitalism through the Protestant ethic. However, Protestantism does accentuate technological progress and hard labor and is like communism as the Christian strives to fulfill his purpose in an historical process limited by time.[32]

Protestantism and communism share a religious and revolutionary asceticism which Luther extended from the monastery to secular society.[33] The Puritans most resembled the communists in this regard, and they also had similar interpretations of destiny, salvation, the role of a vanguard and the continuing struggle against Satan - or class distinctions. Both encouraged man to overcome his limitations - produced by original sin or the lack of proletarian political consciousness - and to see the true way.[34]

Some Protestant movements such as the Diggers, Levellers and True Levellers have been likened to communism as a consequence of their socialistic practices. Crane Brinton labels the Diggers "Biblical communists," and their leader Gerard Winstanley was a predecessor of

Marx in seeing the state as an instrument of class rule.[35] The Anabaptists and Fifth Monarchists have also been cited as having communistic tendencies.[36]

Although the evolution of communism strikingly parallels that of the Catholic Church, the relevance of Protestantism in an historic sense has been increasingly apparent since the Khrushchev period. Concepts of "polycentrism" "national communism" and "different roads to socialism" heve entered into the lexicon of the international communist movement as it has undergone its own Reformation. Domestically, experimentation with capitalist techniques has produced a new variant of the Protestant ethic, and greater diversity within communism bears the attributes of denominationalism.

Jagged Pieces

Many Christians raise valid objections to comparisons of their religion to communism since the two movements have numerous points of divergence despite their similitude. Communist emphasis on class struggle is at variance with Jesus' dictums on loving thy neighbor and thy enemy, and communists tend to express an abstract love for all mankind that neglects love for individuals. Communism views members of certain classes as historically obsolete, whereas Christianity seeks to save the souls of all. Christians even love the heretic, while condemning the heresy.[37]

Christians reject communism's materialism, feeling that it negates man's freedom of action and sense of morality. For them, the dialectic is spiritual - between man and God - and not embedded in the material forces of society. The dialectic also incorporates a supernatural and transcendent quality related to a Creator rather than exibiting close links to progress on earth. The resurrection of Christ symbolizes man's deliverance from history, but communism seeks deliverance within history. It is additionally argued that Christian salvation is individual, whereas communism's is collective, and that Christ's mission is to all men, whereas communism's is solely to the proletariat.[38] Communism is thus a perversion of Christianity which rejects God and Christian grace. A good Christian therefore can not be a communist, but it may be possible to incorporate some aspects of communism into Christianity.[39]

Alongside these criticisms may be placed other points which serve to separate communism from, in particular, Catholicism. Communism has become structurally diffuse, virtually eliminating the authority of the Soviet party's general secretary over communist leaders elsewhere; the Church retains its hierarchical worldwide framework and the pope is the undisputed Vicar of Christ for all Catholics. The Church's loss of much of its secular authority within Italy in the nineteenth and early twentieth centuries has also produced some crucial distinctions from the Communist Party of the Soviet Union, which still rules a superpower. A Catholic can easily leave his Church, but a Soviet communist still lives under the party's control in a secular state even after he has terminated his membership.

Despite these evident differences, comparisons between communism and Christianity are nevertheless instructive as we attempt to understand the essential aspects of religions questing for their own versions of the Kingdom of God. Teleology and eschatology are significant considerations; so are the institutional means of furthering one's cause. Communism and Christianity do indeed have similar bodies proceeding on parallel paths toward concordant ends, but perhaps their souls are ethically incongruous.

Notes

1. Ernst Benz, *Evolution and Christian Hope* (Garden City: Doubleday, 1966), p. 132; Karl Kautsky, *Communism in Central Europe in the Time of the Reformation* (New York: Augustus Kelley, 1966); James Billington, *Fire in the Minds of Men* (New York: Basic Books, 1980), pp. 254-58 and Charles Nordhoff, *The Communistic Societies of the United States* (New York: Dover Publications, 1966).
2. Friedrich Engels, "On the History of Early Christianity," in Lewis Feuer, ed., *Marx and Engels: Basic Writings on Politics and Philosophy* (Garden City: Doubleday, 1959), p. 168; Karl Kautsky, *Foundations of Christianity* (New York: Russell and Russell, 1953), p. 390 and Kautsky, *Communism in Central Europe*, p. 9.
3. Thomas Ogletree in Thomas Ogletree, ed., *Openings for Marxist-Christian Dialogue* (New York: Abingdon Press, 1968), p. 27; Russell Bradner Norris, *God, Marx, and the Future* (Philadelphia: Fortress Press, 1974), pp. 133-34 and Hewlett Johnson, *The Soviet Power* (New York: International Publishers, 1940), p. 319.
4. See Leonardo Boff, *Church: Charism and Power* (New York: Crossroad, 1985), pp. 50 and 52; Richard Lichtman, "The Marxian Critique of Christianity," in Herbert Aptheker, ed., *Marxism and Christianity* (New York: Humanities Press, 1968), pp. 107-108; Jacques Ellul, *The New Demons* (New York: Seabury Press, 1975), pp. 3-6 and Roger Garaudy, *From Anathema to Dialogue* (New York: Herder and Herder, 1966), p. 56.
5. S.F. Kissin, *Farewell to Revolution* (New York: St. Martin's, 1978), p. 34; Benz, pp. 26 and 38 and Leszek Kolakowski, *Toward a Marxist Humanism: Essays on the Left Today* (New York: Grove Press, 1968), p. 174.
6. Donald Smith, *Religion and Political Development* (Boston: Little, Brown, 1970), p. 272; Boff, pp. 52 and 59 and Milan Machovec, *A Marxist Looks at Jesus* (Philadelphia: Fortress Press, 1976), pp. 201-202.
7. Jan Milic Lochman, *Encountering Marx* (Philadelphia: Fortress Press, 1977), p. 42 and Harold Laski, *Faith, Reason and Civilization* (Freeport, New York: Books for Libraries Press, 1972), p. 67.
8. Yuri Furmanov, "Renewing Christ and Marx," *New Times*, no. 22 (May 29-June 4, 1990):32 and Kissin, p. 33.
9. Eugene Kamenka, *The Ethical Foundations of Marxism* (London: Routledge and Kegan Paul, 1962), p. 3.
10. Whittaker Chambers, *Cold Friday* (New York: Random House, 1964), p. 77; Will Herberg, *Faith Enacted as History* (Philadelphia: Fortress Press, 1976), p. 185 and Gustav Wetter, *Dialectical Materialism* (New York: Praeger, 1958), p. 560. John Macmurray, a British philosopher of Marxism, writes: "The main structural principles of Communism are either identical with, or implied in, those of Christianity." See "Christianity and Communism: Towards a Synthesis," in John Lewis, Karl Polanyi and Donald Kitchin, eds., *Christianity and the Social Revolution* (New York: Charles Scribner's Sons, 1936), p. 508.

11 A. Rossi, *A Communist Party in Action* (Hamden, Connecticut: Archon Books, 1970), p. 202; Nicolas Berdyaev, *The Origin of Russian Communism* (Ann Arbor: University of Michigan Press, 1960), p. 153; Reinhold Niebuhr, *Moral Man and Immoral Society* (New York: Charles Scribner's Sons, 1932), p. 257 and John Deedy in John Delaney, ed., *Why Catholic?* (Garden City: Doubleday, 1979), p. 43.
12 Bruce Mazlish, *The Revolutionary Ascetic: Evolution of a Political Type* (New York: McGraw-Hill, 1976), p. 132.
13 For a discussion of the Comintern in a messianic context, see Kermit McKenzie, "The Messianic Concept in the Third International, 1935-1939," in Ernest Simmons, ed., *Continuity and Change in Russian and Soviet Thought* (Cambridge: Harvard University Press, 1955), pp. 516-30.
14 George Orwell, *The Road to Wigan Pier* (London: Secker and Warburg, 1959), p. 177.
15 See Peter Nichols, *The Politics of the Vatican* (New York: Praeger, 1968), p. 132.
16 See Camille Cianfarra, *The Vatican and the Kremlin* (New York: E.P. Dutton, 1950), p. 71.
17 See Nichols, pp. 344-45.
18 Gaston Fessard, "Is Marx's Thought Relevant to the Christian?: A Catholic View," in Nicholas Lobkowicz, ed., *Marx and the Western World* (Notre Dame: University of Notre Dame Press, 1967), p. 363 and Mary-Barbara Zeldin, "The Religious Nature of Russian Marxism," *Journal for the Scientific Study of Religion*, vol. VIII, no. 1 (Spring, 1969):110.
19 Smith, p. 175.
20 See Keith Bridston, *Church Politics* (New York: World Publishing Company, 1969), pp. 149-50.
21 Reinhold Niebuhr, "The Religion of Communism," *Atlantic Monthly*, vol. CXLVI (April, 1931):467; Matthew Spinka, *Christianity Confronts Communism* (New York: Harper and Brothers, 1936), p. 166 and Rene Fueloep-Miller, *The Mind and Face of Bolshevism* (New York: Harper and Row, 1965), p. 280.
22 Lewis Coser, "The Militant Collective: Jesuits and Leninists," *Social Research*, vol. 40, no. 1 (Spring, 1973):112-17.
23 Fueloep-Miller, p. 280; Coser, p. 122 and Ellul, p. 168.
24 Thomas Blakeley, *Soviet Scholasticism* (Dordrecht, Netherlands: D. Reidel, 1961), p. 75 and Wetter, p. 556.
25 Arthur Koestler, *Arrow in the Blue* (New York: Macmillan, 1952), pp. 260 and 288.
26 Wetter, p. 556; Blakeley, pp. 72 and 80; Zeldin, p. 109 and Raymond Aron, *The Opium of the Intellectuals* (New York: W.W. Norton, 1957), p. 287. Erik Erikson writes: "Exegesis was an ideological game which permitted the Church to reinterprtet biblical predictions of its own history according to a new theological line; it was a high form of intellectual and linguistic

exercise; and it provided an oportunity for the display of scholastic virtuosity." See *Young Man Luther* (New York: W.W. Norton, 1958), p. 199.

27 Joseph Bochenski, "Thomism and Marxism-Leninism," *Studies in Soviet Thought*, vol. VII, no. 2 (June, 1967), p. 154.

28 Dale Vree, *On Synthesizing Marxism and Christianity* (New York: John Wiley and Sons, 1976), p. 121 and Rossi, p. 209.

29 Bryan Wilson, *Religion in Secular Society* (Baltimore: Penguin Books, 1966), p. 69; W.T. Stace, *Religion and the Modern Mind* (Philadelphia: Lippincott, 1952), pp. 217-19; Laski, pp. 58-60 and Harold Schilling, *Science and Religion* (New York: Charles Scribner's Sons, 1962), p. 3.

30 Robert V. Daniels, *The Nature of Communism* (New York: Random House, 1962), p. 343; Jeffrey Goldfarb, *Beyond Glasnost* (Chicago: University of Chicago Press, 1989), pp. 43 and 68 and Robert C. Tucker, *The Soviet Political Mind*, revised edition (New York: W.W. Norton, 1971), chapter 7.

31 See Andrew White, *A History of the Warfare of Science With Theology in Christendom* (New York: George Braziller, 1955), pp. 118-56.

32 Benz, pp. 126-28.

33 Mazlish, pp. 50 and 60.

34 Alfred Meyer, *Communism*, third edition (New York: Random House, 1967), pp. 6-9; Michael Walzer, "Puritanism as a Revolutionary Ideology," in Judith Shklar, ed., *Political Theory and Ideology* (New York: Macmillan, 1966), pp. 61-62; Harold Laski, *Reflections on the Revolution of Our Time* (New York: Viking Press, 1943), pp. 74-76; R. Pascal, "Communism in the Middle Ages and Reformation," in Lewis, Polanyi and Kitchin, pp. 121-62 and Joseph Needham, "Land, the Levellers, and the Virtuosi," in Lewis, Polanyi and Kitchin, pp. 163-79.

35 William Hordern, *Christianity, Communism and History* (London: Lutterworth Press, 1957), p. 65; Crane Brinton, *Ideas and Men: The Story of Western Thought*, second edition (Englewood Cliffs: Prentice-Hall, 1963), p. 258 and Eduard Bernstein, *Cromwell and Communism* (New York: Augustus Kelley, 1930), chapter nine.

36 See Hordern, p. 88.

37 Herndon Wagers, "Is Communism a Christian Heresy?," in Merrimon Cuninggim, ed., *Christianity and Communism* (Dallas: Southern Methodist University Press, 1958), p. 93; Jules Monnerot, *Sociology and Psychology of Communism* (Boston: Beacon Press, 1960), p. 281 and Kissin, p. 45.

38 Lester DeKoster, *Communism and Christian Faith* (Grand Rapids: William Eerdmans, 1956), p. 85; Christopher Dawson, *The Dynamics of World History* (New York: New American Library, 1962), p. 356; Aron, p. 274; Wetter, p. 560; Jurgen Moltmann in Ogletree, pp. 51-52; Brinton, p. 379 and Vincent Miceli, *The Gods of Atheism* (New Rochelle, New York: Arlington House, 1971), p. 126.

39 See Lochman, pp. 14-15.

THE SOVIET CHURCH

Chapter X

LAYING THE FOUNDATION

Upon coming to power, the Bolsheviks were not content to await the anticipated withering away of theistic religion but instead took activist measures to speed its demise. Militant atheism was directed against most religious institutions, although there were concurrent efforts to gain control over the Orthodox Church and to ally with Sectarians. The form of atheism adopted was not merely negativistic but had its own structures and rituals and was developed as a new secular religion. With the aid of the "God-builders," a new communist church was institutionalized; it acted intolerantly toward other religions which provided competing sources of belief. Just as Constantine and Theodosius planted Christianity firmly within the Roman Empire, so too did the Bolsheviks turn their version of Marxism into the Soviet state religion. Hierarchy soon came to predominate over egalitarianism as a religion based on humanism and the elimination of alienations headed toward the dark ages of totalitarianism.

Triad

The Bolsheviks formally separated church and state in January 1918 and introduced a new constitution that same year which greatly restricted church ownership of property and denied the right to vote to members of the clergy. Atheist publications and training institutes were established, anti-religious campaigns were set in motion to activate party menbers and vitalize their ideology, and in 1925 the League of the Godless was formed; in 1929, it became the League of the Militant Godless.[1] Numerous churches were closed, some being converted into planetariums, atheist meeting houses or theaters. At one such theater, most of the moviegoers paused to cross themselves near the entrance in deference to an icon of the Virgin Mary that was formerly located there. At the Kremlin, some crosses were replaced with the hammer and sickle; atheist museums were established in Orthodox churches in Leningrad, Catholic churches in Vilnius and Lvov, and in a mosque in Bukhara. An Orthodox monastery even became a stud farm.[2] There was also a campaign against "relic frauds" in order to disprove the saintliness of those whose corpses were preserved. Some supposed corpses were shown to be imitation bodies made of wax, metal or cloth; others that had actually been preserved were shown to have become mummified through the effects of dry air; and others that allegedly were still intact were shown to have rotted.[3]

Metropolitan Tikhon of Moscow was made Patriarch of the Orthodox Church two days before the October Revolution. On February 1, 1918, he anathematized the Bolshevik system; communist party authorities then moved in 1922 to undermine his authority by encouraging the development within Orthodoxy of a "Living Church." To some degree, the "Living Church" represented a rebellion of parish priests against monastic bishops and an accommodation with Bolshevism as opposed to continued loyalty to tsarism. Members of the "Living Church" favored the separation of church and state, believing that the church's divorce from politics could produce a spiritual rebirth.[4] The "Living Church" annulled Tikhon's anathematization of the communist government, condemned him as a counterrevolutionary, and removed him from office. It thus gained legal recognition from the Soviet state in August 1922, and Tikhon was arrested that October.[5]

The "Living Church" declared that the "causes of Lenin and Christ are identical," and deemed capitalism a mortal sin. Supporters were called upon to accept Soviet authority rather than portray it as the Anti-Christ, and it was asserted that only Soviet state power was capable of achieving the ideals of the Kingdom of God. In June 1923, Tikhon repented for his anti-Soviet actions and made his peace with the communist system. He was released from jail and permitted to regain control over the church as its Patriarch. The religious struggle ended with a subservient Orthodox Church so the communists had no reason to continue their backing for the dissident "Living Church" and it soon withered away. Father Sergei, who had sided with the "Living Church," threw his support behind Tikhon and reunified Orthodoxy. Tikhon died in 1925; Sergei became acting Patriarch and was later to be elevated to the post of Patriarch in 1943.[6]

Vladimir Bonch-Bruevich, a close associate of Lenin, has already been cited as the major link between Bolshevism and the Sectarian movement during the pre-revolutionary period. Bonch-Bruevich continued to play this role thereafter and remained a key member of Lenin's inner circle. When Lenin fled to Finnish exile during the July Days of 1917, he stayed at Bonch-Bruevich's home; the night prior to the Bolsheviks' seizure of power in Petrograd, Lenin stayed with Bonch-Bruevich at another of his homes in that city. When Lenin was elected Chairman of the Council of People's Commissars (Sovnarkom) upon overthrowing the Provisional Government, Bonch-Bruevich was appointed the secretary of the Sovnarkom chancellery where he basically functioned as Lenin's personal secretary. It was also Bonch-Bruevich who organized the transferral of the capital from Petrograd to Moscow in March 1918.[7]

In January 1919, Bonch-Bruevich influenced Lenin's decision to exempt Sectarians from military service as long as they had religious motivations and did not operate against the Red Army.[8] In December 1920, a Sectarian was even permitted to address the Eighth Congress of Soviets. Bonch-Bruevich served as Lenin's specialist on the Sectarians. After evaluating the collective nature of Sectarian communes, he recommended that the Bolsheviks encourage Sectarianism; a special government appeal was then made to the Sectarians in October 1921 to organize communes or join those already in existence. In 1924, the communist party praised the Sectarians and moved to assist their agricultural development. That year, Molokan communities in the northern Caucasus joined together to form the "Hammer and Sickle Agricultural Credit Cooperative of United Molokan Communes;" this new collective body included a communist party cell and a branch of the Communist Youth League (Komsomol).[9] Some communes were organized collaboratively by Sectarians and communists: the Flame of the Revolution Commune in the mid-Volga region had two nuns and three communists on its board of directors.[10]

The Sectarians agreed with the Bolsheviks on the separation of church and state as they had been oppressed by tsarism's links to Orthodoxy. They favored a form of Christian socialism, and their views on the status of women and on the unimportance of legal marital bonds were similar to those of the Bolsheviks. Sectarian groups that had split from Orthodoxy such as the Dukhobors, Molokans and Skoptsy were more strongly attracted to the Soviet system than were Western denominations such as the Baptists and Seventh Day Adventists which often differed with the communists on the issues of evolution, abortion, divorce and birth control. Nevertheless, Protestant Sectarians were still given considerable religious freedom during the twenties and the Baptists even organized a youth group modeled on the Komsomol called the Baptomol.[11]

Relations between communists and Sectarians were cordial during the twenties, and many Sectarians joined the communist party. However, differences developed as communes were phased out in favor of the less socialistic artels - the Sectarians complaining that agricultural units were not sufficiently communistic! In addition, the collectivization drive of 1929-33 brought the agricultural sector under greater central control and the practice of religion by the Sectarians was no longer tolerated to the same degree. Also complicating the relationship was the Soviet government's rapprochement with the Orthodox Church, a move viewed suspiciously by the Sectarians.[12]

The Bolsheviks, in a manner comparable to that of the French revolutionaries, suppressed the Christian churches and began to establish a secular religion. In February 1918, the Gregorian calendar replaced the Julian; although Christian in origin, it nevertheless put religious holidays thirteen days out of sync. That same year, the Soviet legislature issued the "Proletarian Ten Commandments" and, on the first anniversary of the October Revolution, Lenin unveiled a statue of Marx and Engels in Red Square.[13] "Red corners" with revolutionary displays were set up in schools, factories and homes and, once Lenin died in January 1924, names such as Vladlen (Vladimir Lenin), Ninel (Lenin spelled backwards), Ilyich (Lenin's patronymic), Melor (Marx, Engels, Lenin and the October Revolution), Vil (Vladimir Ilyich Lenin) and Marlen (Marx and Lenin) were given to Soviet children.

The evolution of the Soviet secular religion will be examined in the ensuing chapters, while the rites of communism will serve as the focus of the current discussion. These rites were opposed by believers in other religions, as well as by those communists who rejected the intrusion of metaphysics and mysticism, but they became widespread during the twenties. After a decline during the Stalin period, they returned with new emphasis under the rule of Nikita Khrushchev.[14]

Secular rites, often mimicking those of Christianity, have been applied to the life cycle from birth to death. "Octobering," instituted during the Civil War, is a form of baptism which can take place at communist party offices or at special baby palaces. Infants are sometimes folded in a red banner and, in the early years after the revolution, they occasionally received a picture of the baby Lenin as a present. Godparents play a role in the ceremony, and parents may be given a calendar with a Soviet hero listed for each day of the year; it is akin to the tradition of saints' days as the names are suggested choices for the newborn.[15] For teenagers, the equivalent of confirmation is the rite for receiving an internal passport at the age of sixteen.

"Red weddings" originated during the twenties, and frequently featured the singing of the Internationale. They gave way to civil wedding ceremonies, which failed to make major inroads in the more religious regions such as Central Asia.[16] In 1959, the first "wedding palace" was opened in Leningrad. Death has not attracted much attention in the communist secular religion as there is no belief in an afterlife. However, a funeral rite was initiated during the sixties in which candles are lit at the gravesite and dirt is thrown on the coffin after it is lowered into the ground.[17]

The communists have parodied church rites by conducting "red masses" at which Christian hymns are sung with the words altered.[18] During the twenties, there were celebrations of "Komsomol Christmas" (the Komsomol is the party youth group) complete with evergreens topped by a red star. In fact, regular Christmas trees were banned from 1928 until 1935 when they were allowed to return under the guise of New Year's trees.[19] During the Christmas season of December 1922-January 1923, an anti-religious counter-Christmas was staged in Moscow which featured Komsomol carols based on Orthodox hymns, skits ridiculing God and the clergy, and the burning of efigies of Jesus, Mohammed, Buddha and other religious figures. Similar observances were held in 416 other towns throughout the country.[20]

The New Year's holiday has been enhanced in importance to compete with Christmas as trees are decorated and Grandfather Frost replaces Santa Claus. Lenin himself participated in a tree lighting ceremony which included Grandfather Frost and a Snow Maiden.[21]

Easter, which has particular importance for the Russian Orthodox, is challenged by rites honoring spring. The Shrovetide prelude to Easter has become Seeing Off of Winter and, in Estonia, Easter eggs have been incorporated into a Day of Birds. Similarly, the Orthodox Whitsun holiday must compete with rites focusing on the birch tree as a fertility symbol for the advent of summer.[22] Thus communism has assumed the function of religion as its earthbound and non-theological rites provide both celebration and solace for the masses.

Return of the "God-Builders"

Efforts to fuse Bolshevism with Sectarianism were short-lived; so too was the "Living Church" which blended Bolshevism and Orthodoxy. The predominant and persisting religious tendency was therefore the development of a new communist secular religion divorced from Christianity, but with rites that echoed Christian themes. The "God-builders" had for long realized that the Soviet masses yearned for religion, and that Bolshevism could be responsive to this spiritual demand. However, Lenin rejected "God-building" and expelled Lunacharsky and Bogdanov from the party. Nevertheless, they were readmitted during the turbulent events of 1917 and again joined with Gorky and Krassin as a "God-building" faction within the Soviet system. Their role at the time of Lenin's death has already been considered, but the influence of these "God-builders" was much broader and must be deemed crucial to the secular religious path taken by the Bolshevik regime.

Aleksandr Bogdanov had a significant impact on the arts through his role as the Moscow director of Proletkult, the organization responsible for disseminating proletarian culture. He was prominent among the founders of Proletkult in 1918, was a featured speaker at Proletkult's first congress in September 1918, and remained active in its affairs until late 1921. Proletkult served as an umbrella for three hundred cultural groups which included a half million participants, and it sponsored thirty-four journals.[23] Bogdanov left Proletkult to concentrate on his blood transfusion experiments, which cost him his life in 1928.

Lunacharsky helped mold Soviet culture from his post as Commissar of Enlightenment, held from October 1917 until 1929 (he died in 1933). Lunacharsky reigned over education as well as culture, and it was his commissariat which subsidized Proletkult. Lunacharsky's tenure as commissar was almost quite brief as he was deeply affected by the damage to the Kremlin caused by Bolsheviks who, shortly after the seizure of power, were trying to round up military cadets still holding out there. He announced his resignation from the Sovnarkom to protest the destruction of culture, but Lenin prevailed upon him to remain a commissar. Lunacharsky (along with Gorky) served as a protector of historic buildings and art, but was unsuccessful in preventing the demolition of ancient churches near the Kremlin.[24]

Lunacharsky hoped to perpetuate revolutionary fervor through public festivals. On May Day of 1918, he organized a celebration at the Winter Palace in Petrograd where a Mozart requiem was played in honor of the martyrs of the October Revolution. His remarks on that occasion were consistent with his "God-building" concepts as he referred to "the judgment on the human personality and its victory in the historical triumph of the idea of humanity."[25]

In 1918, there were two translations into Russian of Campanella's Christian Utopian work *City of the Sun*. Lenin told Lunacharsky that he wanted to apply Campanella's ideas, but base them on Marxist principles. This led to a campaign during the years 1918-21 to construct statues of revolutionary heroes, with Lunacharsky promoting the unveiling of new statues on Sundays - to be accompanied by a celebration of the subject's life. At least fifty such statues were erected, but the program ended in 1921 as there were complaints about the poor quality of workmanship and about the glorification of historical figures.[26]

Maxim Gorky participated in Proletkult and helped intellectuals during the Civil War through assistance with housing and clothing. He was probably the most revered figure in the Soviet arts and "God-building" remained prominent in his thinking as evidenced by his December 1917 allusion to the eventual fusion of all mankind into a common feeling. In the fall of 1927, Gorky referred to man as a "God-builder" who creates miracles, justice and beauty; he averred that there was no force outside of man capable of doing so.[27] In a similar vein, Gorky wrote in 1929: "The Soviet day sings out loudly and to the whole world of the gigantic, heroic and talented work of your class. It sings of the human hero, who gives birth to the collective heroism of the class."[28] In 1934, Gorky commented on the gods of antiquity who had human forms. He claimed that these gods evolved out of social struggle rather than the contemplation of nature, and that they were created by man in his own image. These gods were not abstractions or fantasies but real figures who represented specific labor skills.[29]

Gorky never joined the communist party and did not reside permanently in the Soviet Union. He left for Italy in 1921, returned for visits to his homeland in 1928 and 1930, eventually resettled there in 1932 and died in the Soviet Union four years later. Gorky was nevertheless an imposing figure in Soviet culture, and Stalin initiated a series of meetings with him upon his resumption of residence in 1932. They discussed psychological and literary techniques for studying man, especially the relevance of Pavlovian psychology, and Stalin tried unsuccessfully to recruit Gorky as his biographer.[30] Perhaps Gorky the "God-builder" was reluctant to paeanize Stalin, but his lasting influence on Soviet secular religion helped condition society for the evolving Stalin cult.

Notes

1. See Richard Stites, *Revolutionary Dreams* (New York: Oxford University Press, 1989), chapter five and David Powell, *Antireligious Propaganda in the Soviet Union* (Cambridge: MIT Press, 1975), p. 158.
2. Rene Fueloep-Miller, *The Mind and Face of Bolshevism* (New York: Harper and Row, 1965), p. 186 and Pierre Van Paassen, *Visions Rise and Change* (New York: Dial Press, 1953), p. 73.
3. John Shelton Curtiss, *The Russian Church and the Soviet State, 1917-50* (Boston: Little, Brown, 1953), pp. 85-86 and Fueloep-Miller, p. 187.
4. Curtiss, p. 138 and Fueloep-Miller, pp. 249-50.
5. Kurt Hutten, *Iron Curtain Christians* (Minneapolis: Augsburg, 1967), pp. 17-18 and Matthew Spinka, *The Church in Soviet Russia* (New York: Oxford University Press, 1956), pp. 36-37.
6. Hutten, pp. 17-18; Van Paassen, pp. 278-79; Spinka, pp. 35-36 and 57 and Boleslaw Szczesniak, ed., *The Russian Revolution and Religion* (Notre Dame: University of Notre Dame Press, 1959), p. 92.
7. In 1946, Bonch-Bruevich was appointed as director of an atheist museum in Leningrad. In 1954, he was put in charge of atheistic research within the Academy of Sciences.
8. Bohdan Bociurkiw, "Lenin and Religion," in Leonard Schapiro and Peter Reddaway, eds., *Lenin: the Man, the Theorist, the Leader* (New York: Praeger, 1967), p. 126; Ethel and Stephen Dunn, "Religion as an Instrument of Culture Change: the Problem of the Sects in the Soviet Union," *Slavic Review*, vol. 23 (September, 1964):469 and Robert Wesson, *Soviet Communes* (New Brunswick: Rutgers University Press, 1963), p. 73.
9. Bociurkiw, p. 133; Wesson, p. 75 and the Dunns, p. 470. In December 1919, Commissar of Agriculture S.P. Sereda said that the peasants were religious and therefore receptive to the new communist religion being established within communes. See Wesson, p. 78.
10. Wesson, pp. 73-74.
11. The Dunns, p. 459 and Maurice Hindus, *The Great Offensive* (New York: Harrison Smith and Robert Haas, 1933), pp. 168-72.
12. The Dunns, p. 470 and Wesson, pp. 76 and 208. Some non-Sectarian Christians saw parallels between Christianity and communism and viewed collectivization favorably. In Omsk, several crucifixes were adorned with the hammer and sickle. See Curtiss, pp. 262-64.
13. Nina Tumarkin, *Lenin Lives!: The Lenin Cult in Soviet Russia* (Cambridge: Harvard University Press, 1983), p. 69.
14. See Jennifer McDowell, "Soviet Civil Ceremonies," *Journal for the Scientific Study of Religion*, vol. 13, no. 3 (September, 1974):269.
15. Stites, p. 111 and Christel Lane, *The Rites of Rulers* (Cambridge: Cambridge University Press, 1981), pp. 69-70.
16. Lane, p. 81.
17. Lane, p. 84.

18 Fueloep-Miller, p. 191.
19 Stites, pp. 230-31.
20 Stites, p. 109; Curtiss, pp. 202-203 and McDowell, p. 266.
21 Lane, p. 137.
22 Lane, pp. 131, 134 and 136-37.
23 Stites, p. 71.
24 Sheila Fitzpatrick, *The Commissariat of Enlightenment* (London: Cambridge University Press, 1970), p. 89 and Stites, p. 243.
25 Stites, p. 84.
26 Stites, p. 88.
27 Bertram Wolfe, *The Bridge and the Abyss* (New York: Praeger, 1967), pp. 52-53.
28 Katerina Clark, "Little Heroes and Big Deeds: Literature Responds to the First Five-Year Plan," in Sheila Fitzpatrick, ed., *Cultural Revolution in Russia, 1928-1931* (Bloomington: Indiana University Press, 1978), p. 205.
29 Maynard Solomon, *Marxism and Art* (New York: Knopf, 1973), p. 244.
30 David Joravsky, "The Construction of the Stalinist Psyche," in Fitzpatrick, *Cultural Revolution in Russia*, pp. 126-27 and Robert McNeal, *Stalin: Man and Ruler* (New York: N.Y.U. Press, 1988), p. 149.

Chapter XI

THE MEDIEVAL EDIFICE

Stalinism represented the Middle Ages of communist development. Soviet church power was centralized; the "papacy" was strengthened through the institutionalization of the post of General Secretary; Crusades and an Inquisition were carried out against infidels and heretics; and the ruling communist party came to control intellectual life through its dominance over universities and publishing. The party additionally asserted its power over the economy and organized the peasants into collectives, just as the medieval Church became the largest possessor of wealth and benefited from serfdom.[1]

Stalin's primacy in Soviet politics was reminiscent of the ascendancy of papal theocracy. In 1073, Pope Gregory VII wrote that the Church had never erred and would never do so, that the pope could not be judged by others, and that his judgments could only be revised by himself.[2] In the twelfth century, the image of popes was enhanced as they came to be called Vicars of Christ rather than Vicars of Peter. In the Soviet Union, Stalin became revered as the leading Marxist-Leninist, the "vozhd" or supreme leader of his people, and as the Generalissimo guiding Mother Russia through the Second World War. His powers became absolute as the Soviet communist church built upon its foundations in a pyramidal and hierarchical manner.

The Stalinist Religion

Stalinism has been called a "religious phenomenon," a form of "religious worship," "laicized theology," "sacrosanct dogma," and "sectarian fanaticism."[3] Polish philosopher Leszek Kolakowski subscribes to such an interpretation, witness this description of the late Stalin period: "All the forms of popular religiosity were revived in a distorted shape: icons, processions, prayers recited in chorus, confession of sins (under the name of self-criticism), the cult of relics. Marxism in this way became a parody of religion, but one devoid of content."[4]

Stalinism had a religious quality as it evolved from the Soviet secular religion developed by Lenin and the "God-builders." However, there are more direct causes attributable to Stalin the individual, a man who was strongly influenced by Orthodoxy as a youth. Stalin's mother was highly devout and it appears that when Yosif was three or four, she moved with him into the household of an Orthodox priest named Charkviani in order to gain employment as a servant. Yosif was raised under these conditions for about ten years, during which he also attended religious primary and secondary schools in his home town of Gori. He then studied at an Orthodox seminary in Tbilisi for five years, where he gained a reputation as a serious scholar of religion and a strong believer in the church's theology.[5] It is therefore not surprising that Stalin developed a speaking style with overtones of the catechism as he often asked rhetorical questions and then incorporated these questions into his answers. He also had repetitive diction and frequently used a Christian frame of reference. When criticized by the commander of the Moscow military district at the Fifteenth Party Congress in December 1927, Stalin said forgive them their sins for they know not what they are saying.[6] Stalin exhibited a Manichaean mindset often associated with early Christianity, and he tended to view those who disagreed with him as heretics.[7]

Lenin opposed "God-building," and the Lenin cult gathered momentum only after his death; in fact, it was the date of his death that assumed religious prominence within the cult. In the case of Stalin, the personality cult clearly evolved during his lifetime and it was his date of birth that became the focus of celebration.[8] Petrograd did not become Leningrad until after Lenin's death, but Tsaritsyn was renamed Stalingrad in 1925, only a year after Lenin's demise. As portrayed by Soviet historian Roy Medvedev, Stalin did not follow Lenin in rejecting "God-building" but instead established a socialist religion which included a god: "And the all-powerful, all-knowing, all-holy god of the new religion was himself, Stalin." French political sociologist Raymond Aron refers to the "transfiguration of a man."[9]

The Stalin cult was given some impetus by the lavish praise bestowed upon the Soviet leader on his fiftieth birthday in December 1929, but an examination of school texts published during the years 1930-32 indicates that Stalin had not yet achieved cult status. According to James Heizer, who has closely scrutinized the Stalin cult, its full-blown manifestations first became evident in 1932 and school texts began to reflect this phenomenon in 1933. Photos of Stalin also came to be featured more prominently in *Pravda* during this latter year, and the title of "vozhd" was assumed by Stalin in 1934.[10] As the Stalin cult grew, the Lenin cult was downplayed. Stalin's treatment of Lenin's widow demonstrates this development as Stalin attended Krupskaya's funeral in 1939 but failed to deliver a eulogy. Her writings were then suppressed.[11]

Songs about Stalin were sung by school children like morning prayers, and he was often referred to in the arts as the sun; the old religious term "Joseph Bright" was also applied. Socialist realism, which could be likened to church art, glorified Stalin; a 1950 joint painting by three artists, entitled "Glory to the Great Stalin," depicted him with twelve followers who clearly were reminiscent of the apostles.[12] Late Stalinist art has aptly been described as "ecclesiastical" and as suggesting "a unification of two utopias: Heavenly Jerusalem and Communist Society."[13]

Stalin came to be portrayed as an immortal and infallible leader, and his cult was extended to fields in which he was supposedly a genius such as the sciences, psychology and linguistics. The apogee of this cult was achieved on the occasion of Stalin's seventieth birthday in 1949 when he was lavished with praise; the writer Leonid Leonov proposed that, in the future, a new calendar could be created which would number the years from the date of Stalin's birth.[14]

Stalin died on March 5, 1953 and his body, like Lenin's, was put on display in the Hall of Columns. Following his March 9 funeral, Stalin was laid to rest in Lenin's mausoleum as Soviet communism's second embalmed saint.

Hidden Demons

The communist religion under Stalin sought to identify "kulaks," "wreckers" and "cosmopolitans" who were charged with operating clandestinely against the true faith. Scapegoats were needed to account for communist policy failures, and a devil theory was presented which claimed to identify "ubiquitous, insidious, powerful and morally corrosive" forces which were well-disguised when carrying out their evil deeds. Such Satanic influences had to be elimninated from society in order to purge it of a potentially fatal poison.[15] Through an inverse logic, the party's failures were depicted as the result of policy correctness: otherwise, why would these negative anti-communist agents try to subvert the party's policies?[16] Beginning with the Shakhty affair in 1928, which led to the execution of five defendants, false charges were leveled against supposed enemies of the people; this process then culminated in the Great Purge and the Moscow show trials of the thirties.[17]

The Russian folk belief in "spoiling" is based on malevolent beings such as witches or sorcerers who are blamed for illnesses allegedly caused in many instances by the alteration of food or drink. During the seventeenth century, illnesses of royal family members were often attributed to such witchcraft and, if a defendant had pleaded guilty to the charges, he would be pressured to reveal a broader conspiracy including other purported witches.[18] This cultural tradition continued into the Soviet period. At the 1938 show trial known as the "Trial of Twenty-one," defendants were accused of murders committed through improper medical care and the administration of poisons. It was claimed by the prosecution that Gorky and his son had died in this manner, as well as high government officials Valerian Kuibyshev and Vyacheslav Menzhinsky.[19] Kremlin doctors stood among the accused, an interesting circumstance in light of the arrest of Kremlin doctors in January 1953 on the same trumped up charge of killing Soviet leaders through medical malfeasance. In this latter instance, known as the "doctors' plot," it was alleged that Andrei Zhdanov's death in 1948 had been caused by such inappropriate treatment. A curious sub-theme throughout these witchhunts was anti-Semitism as most of the accused doctors were Jewish. This is reminiscent of the period leading up to the Spanish Inquisition when rumors were spread that Jewish doctors were permitting Christian patients to die. In 1335 and 1412, laws were decreed threatening Christians with excommunication for using the services of Jewish doctors.[20]

Trotsky was the arch-enemy of the Stalinist religion, the anti-Soviet Anti-Christ. He was depicted as the evil figure lurking behind the show trial defendants, a demon who had to be exorcized. He basically represented a psychological threat to Stalinism since there was actually no reputable evidence that he was in fact trying to subvert the Soviet system. As a Jew, it was not difficult to arouse public anti-Semitic passions against him as anti-Semitism had been deply ingrained in the Soviet Union's Slavic cultures since tsarist times. In 1940, Trotsky eventually fell victim in Mexico to a Stalinist assassin armed with a mountain climbing pick.

Upholding the Faith

Medieval Christendom featured Crusades and an Inquisition against enemies of the faith. Pope Gregory VII planned the First Crusade, but it was actually launched by Urban II during the years 1095-99. The aim was to assert Christian control of Jerusalem in preparation for the Kingdom of God, and Crusades took place through the year 1291. Christian authority was imposed on Jerusalem for the period 1099-1187, but the Moslems reassumed control and the Crusades ended in failure. In a similar manner, the Communist International (Comintern) was unsuccessful in overthrowing capitalist systems. The Hungarian communist regime of 1919 lasted for only four months, and four attempts at revolution in Germany were effectively suppressed. Like the Crusades, the Comintern tried to mobilize internationally against the "infidels;" this was especially evident in China and Spain where numerous agents of diverse nationalities were deployed to counter the ideological foe.

The possession of a perceived absolute truth tends to produce a search for heresy. In 1215, the Lateran Council under the leadership of Pope Innocent III started the Inquisition. The machinery for its operation, including the appointment of inquisitors to sit in Florence, was developed by Gregory IX after becoming pope in 1227. The well-known Spanish Inquisition came considerably later. Initiated by Ferdinand and Isabella in 1480, it led to the expulsion of the Jews in 1492 and of Moorish Moslems in 1501. In 1609, even those Moors who had adopted Christianity (Moriscos) were evicted from Spain.

Stalinism closely resembled the Inquisition. The Great Purge was known as a "cleansing," implying a religious purification, as alleged heretics were forced to recant their errors. Society was being prepared for socialism so a resurgence of class enemies was being unleashed just as Satan was seen as working against the advent of the Kingdom of God. On Easter eve of 1929, a Soviet play condemned the Inquisition as an exhibition of religious excess and members of the Pioneers, a party youth group, chased the inquisitors from the stage.[21] Six years later, the communist religious system began to devour its own as a large number of people became expendable in order to advance the faith.[22] Whereas the Inquisition was ostensibly aimed at saving individual souls from damnation, Stalinism was (on the theoretical level) more concerned with saving man collectively. The Soviet purge thus subordinated personal salvation to the fear that erring souls would have a contaminating effect on others, an outlook sure to produce the application of terror.[23]

Terror was therefore used to promote faith, and belief was further divorced from reason. It was emphasized, a la Christian martyrdom, that religious predecessors had died for their faith rather than renounce or modify it; on the other hand, ideologically suspect party members who attempted to cite Marx or Lenin as justification for their views were ironically declared disloyal to Stalin and subjected to punishment or death. Such an approach harkens back to Christianity during the Middle Ages where the Bible was kept from the faithful so its concepts could not be cited in challenges to ecclesiastical authority. The revolutionary generation of Soviet leadership was paradoxically eliminated in order to further the revolution; Lenin's closest associates were executed following show trials in the Hall of Columns, the place where the body of Vladimir Ilyich had lain in state.[24]

The Inquisition and Soviet purges were similar in that defendants usually were not told who were their accusers, they were compelled to testify against themselves, their relatives were forced to testify as well, and there was no right of appeal. Confessions were sought as guilt had to be justified despite flimsy evidence and unreliable witnesses. Those who confessed could also be used as witnesses against other defendants. The accused had great difficulty in presenting witnesses on his or her behalf as they could fall victim to the purge through charges of being accomplices to heresy.[25] The Soviet practice paralleled the Catholic tradition as the denial of sin is deemed worse than sin, and a sinner who denies his acts cannot be redeemed.[26]

In the Inquisition, there was a ceremony known as the "sermo generalis" in which confessions were read and convicted heretics had to confirm them prior to sentencing. At Soviet show trials, there were similar recantations, which sometimes gained a waiver of the death penalty. Torture was authorized by Pope Innocent IV in 1252 and was widespread during the Soviet purges. It was aimed at securing confessions, which were generally based on falsifications offered solely to have the maltreatment terminated.[27] Thus torture did not engender truth, but it helped perpetuate a belief system ostensibly grounded in absolutism.

The communist party portrayed itself as infallible and attempted to justify the purges on the basis of its wisdom being somewhat unfathomable to the masses. Applying a "Book of Job theory," the party depicted suffering as a test of the populace that could only strengthen the true believers.[28] Some victims of torture refused to accept that such acts could have been approved by higher party authorities and they displayed their loyalty by writing in blood on their cell walls, "Long Live Stalin!"[29] Others maintained their faith in the party because they had for long participated in its activities; renouncing allegiance would therefore imply that their party years had been spent in vain.[30] Nikolai Bukharin explained at his show trial in 1938 that he decided to confess because he needed some cause for which to die; he therefore tried to identify positive aspects of the communist party, even though it was bringing about his execution.[31]

An interesting perspective is provided by the account of Mikhail Yakubovich, who was convicted of "wrecking" in 1931 despite his innocence. He quotes the prosecutor N.V. Krylenko, who told him privately before the trial: "I have no doubt that you personally are not guilty of anything. We are both performing our duty to the Party - I have considered and consider you a Communist. I will be the prosecutor at the trial, you will confirm the testimony given during the investigation. This is our duty to the Party, yours and mine." Yakubovich gave false testimony to help convict himself, and felt so guilty for doing so that he hoped to die. He confessed to his alleged crimes, and did not request that his life be spared. It was, nevertheless.[32]

Under the Thumb

Stalin furthered the atheistic communist religion, but he also secured the support of Orthodoxy as he promoted nationalistic themes. The Orthodox Church became subservient to the party and permitted itself to be used to advance the causes of the Soviet system. In return, Orthodox authorities retained their posts.

In July 1927, Acting Patriarch Sergei called for submission to the "lawful government" and he religiously endorsed Soviet rule by declaring: "People have forgotten that for a Christian there are no fortuitous events, and that what has occurred in our land, as everywhere and at all times, has been the work of God's providence, undeviatingly leading every nation toward its predestined goal."[33] Church-state peace then prevailed throughout the thirties as Stalin carried out a nationalist revival in preparation for an anticipated war with Germany. Tsarist history was again recognized as part of the national heritage, Ivan the Terrible was elevated to the status of national hero, army officers were given enhanced privileges, and laws were adjusted so as to strengthen the family. During this period, a school of icon painters was brought in to restore church artworks within the Kremlin.[34]

The Second World War produced a display of national unity between Orthodoxy and the communist party. Stalin gestured toward the Christian faithful by suspending publication of the leading atheist journal *Bezbozhnik* in September 1941; he later established an Order of Aleksandr Nevsky for patriotism in 1942, named for a man who had been sainted in 1380. Sergei, who had been Acting Patriarch since 1925, was permitted to assume the title of Patriarch in September 1943; he had an audience with Stalin that same month. Stalin then ordered repairs to the entrance to the Gate of the Redeemer in the Kremlin, which had suffered bullet hole damage around an icon in 1917.[35] Patriarch Sergei died in May 1944, and Acting Patriarch Aleksei immediately called Stalin "a wise God-appointed leader."[36] In February 1945, he was enthroned as Patriarch after the Orthodox Church had sent a message to the Soviet government on January 31 praising Stalin and asserting that it was receiving complete government cooperation in its work.[37] The following year, the Ukrainian Orthodox Church was placed under the authority of the Orthodox Church, thus severing its administrative affiliation with the Vatican.

In November 1947, in commemoration of the thirtieth anniversary of the October Revolution, Patriarch Aleksei released the following message to be read in all Orthodox churches: "We shall redouble our prayers for the God-protected Russian state and for its authorities at whose head is the wise leader, whom the providence of God chose to put to lead our fatherland on the path of prosperity and glory."[38] In July 1948, the Orthodox Church Conference in Moscow passed a resolution which obliquely portrayed Orthodoxy as the defender of the workers, the weak and the exploited in opposition to the Roman Catholic Church, which was negatively portrayed as allied with the strong.[39]

Stalin gave special rights to the Orthodox Church, but always managed to keep it subservient as he advanced his own communist religion. The Soviet Union passed through its own Middle Ages of dominant church authority; then Stalin died and the country experienced a Renaissance and Reformation.

Notes

1. See Richard Lichtman, "The Marxian Critique of Christianity," in Herbert Aptheker, ed., *Marxism and Christianity* (New York: Humanities Press, 1968), pp. 107-108.
2. R.W. Southern, *Western Society and the Church in the Middle Ages* (Grand Rapids, Michigan: William Eerdman's, 1970), p. 102.
3. Stephen Cohen, *Rethinking the Soviet Experience* (New York: Oxford University Press, 1985), p. 101; Roy Medvedev, *On Socialist Democracy* (New York: Knopf, 1975), p. 346; Roger Garaudy, *The Alternative Future* (New York: Simon and Schuster, 1974), pp. 82-83 and Robert Tucker, "The Rise of Stalin's Personality Cult," *The American Historical Review*, vol. 84, no. 2 (April, 1979):352.
4. Leszek Kolakowski, *Main Currents of Marxism*, vol. 3 (Oxford: Clarendon Press, 1978), p. 147.
5. See Robert McNeal, *Stalin: Man and Ruler* (New York: NYU Press, 1988), pp. 2-4.
6. Richard Crossman, ed., *The God That Failed* (New York: Bantam, 1954), p. 47 and *Moskovskaya Pravda*, September 18, 1987 (FBIS - SOV-87-186, September 25, 1987, p. 48).
7. George Urban, ed., *Stalinism* (New York: St. Martin's, 1982), p. 130 and James Heizer, "The Cult of Stalin, 1929-1939," doctoral dissertation, University of Kentucky, 1977, p. 198.
8. See Isaac Deutscher, *Ironies of History: Essays on Contemporary Communism* (London: Oxford University Press, 1966), p. 181.
9. Roy Medvedev, *Let History Judge* (New York: Knopf, 1971), p. 151 and Raymond Aron, *The Opium of the Intellectuals* (New York: W.W. Norton, 1957), p. xiii.
10. Heizer, pp. 58, 102-103 and 105-106. Stalin was called "vozhd" for the first time at the 1933 May Day celebration in an address by Voroshilov.
11. Robert McNeal, "Krupskaia: the Feminine Subcult," in Bernard Eissenstat, ed., *Lenin and Leninism* (Lexington: Lexington, 1971), p. 224.
12. Anton Antonov-Ovseyenko, *The Time of Stalin: Portrait of a Tyranny* (New York: Harper and Row, 1981), p. 229; Richard Stites, *Revolutionary Dreams* (New York: Oxford University Press, 1989), pp. 248-49 and Lars Erik Blomqvist, "Some Utopian Elements in Stalinist Art," *Russian History*, vol. 11, nos. 2-3 (Summer-Fall, 1984):305.
13. Blomqvist, p. 301.
14. Antonov-Ovseyenko, p. 227.
15. Gregor Sebba, "Symbol and Myth in Modern Rationalistic Societies," in Thomas Altizer, William Beardslee and J. Harvey Young, eds., *Truth, Myth and Symbol* (Englewood Cliffs: Prentice-Hall, 1962), pp. 154-56.
16. See Adam Ulam, *Stalin* (New York: Viking, 1973), p. 303.
17. See Medvedev, *Let History Judge*, chapter IV.

18. Linda Ivanits, *Russian Folk Belief* (Armonk, New York: M.E. Sharpe, 1989), p. 129 and Russell Zguta, "Witchcraft Trials in Seventeenth-Century Russia," *American Historical Review*, vol. 82, no. 5 (December 1977):1192-93.
19. See McNeal, *Stalin*, p. 206.
20. John O'Brien, *The Inquisition* (New York: Macmillan, 1973), p. 95.
21. Christel Lane, *The Rites of Rulers* (Cambridge: Cambridge University Press, 1981), pp. 175-76.
22. See Lewis Coser, "Millenarians, Totalitarians and Utopians," *Dissent*, vol. 5, no. 1 (Winter, 1958):70.
23. Margaret Mead, *Soviet Attitudes Toward Authority* (New York: William Morrow, 1951), p. 23.
24. Urban, pp. 129-31; O'Brien, p. 6 and Kolakowski, pp. 85-86.
25. See O'Brien, pp. 12-13 and 18.
26. From a somewhat different perspective, Archbishop Fulton Sheen has explained that if one is blind and denies the existence of light, one will never be able to see. Presented in John Delaney, ed., *Why Catholic?* (Garden City: Doubleday, 1979), pp. 181-82.
27. Kolakowski, p. 87.
28. F. Beck and W. Godin, *Russian Purge and ther Extraction of Confession* (New York: Viking, 1951), p. 227.
29. Yevgeny Yevtushenko, *A Precocious Autobiography* (London: Collins and Harvill, 1963), p. 13.
30. Urban, p. 424. Yugoslav dissident Milovan Djilas describes his recantation following charges against him in 1954: "The fateful crux of the matter lay in my emotional attitude. I continued to feel that I was a Communist, albeit hesitant about certain dogmas, that I was bound body and soul to the Communist party. Like the heretics of days gone by, like the sundry oppositionists in the Stalin trials, I proved my loyalty to the ideology and to the party by recantation." See *The Unperfect Society: Beyond the New Class* (New York: Harcourt, Brace and World, 1969), p. 244.
31. Hugo Dewar, *The Modern Inquisition* (London: Allan Wingate, 1953), p. 38.
32. Medvedev, *Let History Judge*, pp. 130-31.
33. Matthew Spinka, *The Church in Soviet Russia* (New York: Oxford University Press, 1956), p. 163.
34. Lane, p. 125.
35. Pierre Van Paassen, *Visions Rise and Change* (New York: Dial Press, 1955), pp. 317 and 321.
36. Spinka, p. 107.
37. *Moscow News*, February 7, 1945.
38. *Journal of the Moscow Patriarchate*, no. 11 (November, 1947). In this same issue, an article by Antonina Shapovalova relates equality before the law in the Soviet system to the church belief in equality before God.
39. TASS, July 23, 1948.

Chapter XII

FROM RENAISSANCE TO COUNTER-REFORMATION

At the time of Stalin's death in March 1953, the Soviet political system lacked the Vatican's mechanism for selecting new popes which had been developed at the Lateran Council of 1179. There was no clear succession procedure, engendering a power struggle that was eventually won by Nikita Khrushchev. Khrushchev and his fellow survivors of Stalinist terror terminated the latest phase of the Inquisition, in the form of the "doctors' plot," and ushered in a more humane period which may be compared to the Renaissance. Greater freedom within the communist bloc soon produced a Reformation challenging Soviet dominance, leading Khrushchev into a Counter-Reformation that later became more pronounced during the Brezhnev period. Domestically, this freedom came to undermine Khrushchev's own authority as he was removed from power in a peaceful and institutional manner in October 1964. Although Khrushchev was similar to many popes of the fifteenth and sixteenth centuries, he differed to the extent that he at first encouraged the Protestantization of his own church through advocacy of de-Stalinization and different roads to socialism. The forces unleashed then exceeded his regulative capabilities, producing his downfall and a virulent Sino-Soviet conflict.

The Human Factor

Renaissance popes, especially Nicholas V (1447-55), went along with the new intellectual currents and became patrons of the rising intelligentsia through the establishment of libraries.[1] They recognized the Renaissance's mistrust of the medieval Church's world outlook, but were consoled by the return to original Christian sources of knowledge. Khrushchev likewise presided over the "Thaw" in Soviet culture as central controls were relaxed and the creative arts began to flourish. Stalinist repression was condemned, and submerged antagonism to totalitarian methods was permitted to rise to the surface. In October 1962, Yevgeny Yevtushenko's poem "Stalin's Heirs" warned about the former autocrat's legacy; the following month, the journal *Novy Mir* published Aleksandr Solzhenitsyn's *One Day in the Life of Ivan Denisovich*, a searing indictment of Stalinist labor camps. Khrushchev indicated that he had personally approved both works. He became a proponent of limited humanistic reform in the arts as there was a turn away from officially sponsored socialist realism. In some ways, Khrushchev may be likened to Desiderius Erasmus who helped widen the bounds of the Renaissance in the Netherlands. He freed Soviet intellectuals from many bureaucratic and ideological shackles, and also initiated extensive cultural exchanges with the West.

Khrushchev, unlike Stalin, mingled with Soviet citizens and normalized party operations by having its organs meet regularly according to the rules and by permitting debate at sessions of the party's highest policy-making forum, the Presidium. He also injected some humanism by demoting opponents rather than executing them, and he attempted to combat entrenched bureaucratization by calling for a periodic turnover of party personnel. In a manner reminiscent of the Reformation, Khrushchev's growing acceptance of individualism was linked to greater economic liberty and decentralization. So-called "goulash communism," with its emphasis on consumer goods, became the keynote and the central authorities turned over many planning functions to industrial managers and considerable administrative responsibility to regional economic councils known as "sovnarkhozy."

Khrushchev moved to eradicate the remnants of Soviet medievalism through the process of de-Stalinization. This paralleled the Catholic Church's own reformist policies of the early sixteenth century, and the Protestant Reformationist tide of that era which raised skepticism about sainthood and religious relics.[2] The de-iconization and mortalization of Stalin began with medical bulletins as he lay dying, followed by an autopsy. Stalin's name was no longer applied to the Soviet constitution, and Stalin prizes were not awarded in the spring of 1953. His last book, *Economic Problems of Socialism in the U.S.S.R.*, was removed from the reading list at party ideological schools.³ Stalin's image was somewhat revived in mid-1953, only to be tarnished permanently by Khrushchev's "secret speech" to the Twentieth Congress of the C.P.S.U. in February 1956.

The denigration of Stalin was accompanied by renewed glorification of Lenin. On the April 22, 1953 anniversary of Lenin's birth, *Pravda* published an article on "The Great Life-Affirming Force of Leninism;" in 1955, celebrations honoring Lenin were switched from the January 21 date of his death to the April birthday. "Lenin corners" again became popular, and new biographies of Lenin were often hagiographical works in the format of the gospels.⁴ Krupskaya also was the recipient of renewed attention as a revolutionary heroine.

Stalin's body was embalmed upon his death and placed within the Red Square mausoleum next to Lenin. A joint March 7, 1953 decree by the party's Central Committee and the Council of Ministers called for the construction of a pantheon for Lenin, Stalin and other political figures, but the Soviet media did not mention this plan again until July 4, 1954. An architectural contest was announced to plan the new mausoleum in the Lenin hills three and a half kilometers south of Moscow State University. The deadline for entries was set at November 1, but the entire undertaking was relegated to oblivion and Stalin's sarcophagus remained in Red Square.⁵

The anti-Stalin campaign reached a climax in October 1961 at the time of the Twenty-second Congress of the C.P.S.U.. Delegations from several factories, including the one at which Lenin was wounded in a 1918 assassination attempt, introduced resolutions calling for the removal of Stalin's body from the mausoleum. A delegate named Dora Lazurkina created the greatest stir with her account of Lenin's appearance in a vision and his request to have Stalin's corpse distanced from his own. In her words, she "took counsel with Ilyich and he stood before me as though alive."⁶ On October 31, Stalin was buried alongside the Kremlin wall in a simple grave; embalming of his body was no longer sustained as he was reduced to the status of a mere mortal ("No, Stalin has not given up. He thinks he can outsmart death. We carried him from the mausoleum. But how carry Stalin's heirs away from Stalin" - Yevgeny Yevtushenko, "Stalin's Heirs").

De-Stalinization produced a "crisis of faith" as questions arose about the nature of the Soviet system and its ideology. If the man praised as infallible and the greatest Marxist-Leninist for almost three decades was actually a tyrant and intellectual buffoon, then surely many aspects of

Soviet society were a sham built on coercion and falsity.[7] Communism came under critical scrutiny, resulting in serious challenges to central Soviet authority through the rise of a new Reformation.

Reformation in Red

The doctrinal rigidity and emphasis on absolute truth exhibited during the Stalin period was inextricably linked to the monolithic political structure developed within the Soviet bloc; as ideological doubts grew, communist cohesion fell victim as fissiparous nationalist tendencies gained momentum.[8] It is surely not accidental that Khrushchev's "secret speech" attacking Stalin was followed rapidly by revolutions in Poland and Hungary, and by probing questions about the Soviet system raised by the Italian communist leader Palmiro Togliatti.[9] Communism was breaking up into national churches and, with the decline of central ideological guidance from Moscow, unity in the theoretical sphere could only be achieved by verbal gymnastics and appeals to the lowest common denominator, as in the Twelve Party Declaration of November 1957 and the Eighty-one Party Statement of December 1960.[10]

During the sixteenth century princes challenged the secular authority of the Vatican as the Reformation was, to a great extent, a reaction to central control.[11] In the Soviet bloc, the Reformation may appropriately be associated with Khrushchev but it was already presaged at the end of Stalin's rule by the 1948 break between the Soviet Union and Yugoslavia. The causes of this controversy were more nationalistic than doctrinal, and Yugoslavia's steps along its own road to socialism may justly be compared to those taken by the national churches which defied Rome.[12] The Catholic Church lost Germany, Britain, the Scandinavian countries and the Netherlands; the Soviet church witnessed the defections of Yugoslavia, China and Albania. In both cases, states were the key actors in moving their societies toward a new religious vision. The Peace of Westphalia in 1648 gave recognition to the state-centric order in international relations, which signified the diminution of religious influence over secular authority. In the communist world, Moscow's leading role gave way to "polycentrism." The communist movement, however, did attempt to work out basic differences at the Eighty-one Party Conference of November-December 1960; Protestant calls for reconciliation at a general council were rejected by Pope Clement VII.

The Reformation, in common with the Chinese challenge to the Soviets in the late fifties and early sixties, was not aimed at promoting religious diversity but at identifying the true religious path. The Catholic Church, and communist leaders in the Kremlin, were seen as neglectful of spirituality and too concerned with matters of power and privilege. A return to original roots was therefore advocated, with an emphasis on scripture rather than church authority. The Bible, and the classics of Marxism-Leninism, were to serve as the basis of a renewed religiosity as allegiance to the values of the original church was to be accentuated.[13] Skepticism was eschewed as the divinity of Christ was not questioned, nor was the scientific basis of Leninism. The Chinese communists claimed fealty to ideology, and labeled their spring 1960 campaign against perceived Soviet apostasy "Long Live Leninism!' The Soviets were accused of forsaking their communist religion for "revisionism," whereas the Chinese believed that they were the ideological heirs of Marx and Lenin. As in the Reformation, those who rebeled against church authority did not claim to be innovators but rather blamed the church itself for innovations leading away from essential doctrine and practice.[14]

The Chinese communists resembled Martin Luther as they opposed church politics, but not the church.[15] They wanted to reform the church, not create a new one, and did not establish rival institutions to compete with those dominated by the Soviet Union. At the Twelve Party Conference of November 1957 and the Eight-one Party Conference of November-December 1960, the Chinese worked with the Soviets to reconcile differences within the communist movement. At the same time they worked to limit Moscow's authority, and their portrayal of Khrushchev was similar to Luther's depiction of popes as Anti-Christs. Ideologically, the Communist Party of China sought to combat perceived Soviet deviations from Marxism-Leninism; the Twenty-five Points of June 1963 may thus be compared to Luther's Ninety-five Theses of October 1517.

The Chinese, along with their Albanian allies, were "thin" communists and therefore representative of the more ascetic, revolutionary and materially deprived wing of the communist movement. Mao Zedong, as Luther, was of peasant background and he likewise railed against luxury and praised hard work. Mao condemned the materialism and entrenched bureaucracy evident in the Soviet Union, and his claim that quantity (in the form of labor) could be substituted for quality(the economic base) was an attempt to stress the Chinese commitment to a revolutionary work ethic. China, as in the Great Leap Forward of 1958, was to organize its enormous manpower to compensate for its technological deficiencies.

Reformationist Protestant themes of strict morality and rigorous discipline, as practiced by the Anabaptists, are germane to the Chinese and Albanian challenges to Moscow. Anabaptism, as representative of the Reformation's left wing, has been compared to the Albanian system;[16] its belief that baptism was insufficient to make one a Christian as faith had to be experienced as an adult could well be related to China's Cultural Revolution of 1966 with its emphasis on young people being integrated into the revolutionary process. China and Albania developed variants of the communist religion, but were no less doctrinaire than the Soviet communists as they sought their own versions of absolute truth. As the Calvinist Theodore Beza observed, religious liberty is "a most diabolical dogma because it means that every one should be left to go to hell in his own way."[17]

Countering the Tide

Nikita Khrushchev, the man who opened the floodgates to the Soviet Renaissance and the international communist Reformation, also presided over the initiation of the Soviet Counter-Reformation. Although he continued to permit some artistic and intellectual leeway, he moved to strengthen the role of ideology by sponsoring the 1959 publication of *Fundamentals of Marxism-Leninism* and the administrative role of the communist party by establishing separate divisions responsible for industry and agriculture. In intra-bloc affairs, he accepted Yugoslavia's alternative path to communism but sought to impose limits on autonomy by threatening intervention in Poland in 1956, invading Hungary that same year, and expelling Albania from the bloc in 1961.[18] When he was removed from power in October 1964, he was planning an international communist meeting that may have ejected China.

Khrushchev predicted that the goal of a communist society could be achieved by 1980, and he enhanced the authority of the Soviet communist church by furthering secular religion at the expense of theological credos. A university of atheism was founded in Ashkhabad, Turkmen in 1958; the atheistic journal *Nauka i Religiya* (Science and Religion) was inaugurated in 1959; and an anti-religious campaign over the years 1959-64 led to the shutting down of 14,000 of the 22,000 remaining Orthodox churches and 5 0f 8 theological seminaries.[19] Numerous monasteries and convents were also closed, and a Znanie (Knowledge) Society was formed in 1963 to promote atheistic values.

Khrushchev encouraged considerable literary freedom through the fall of 1962, but conservatives who preferred a cultural Counter-Reformation managed to gain the first secretary's support later that year. Khrushchev was known to be critical of modern art so they made sure that he visited the Manezh exhibit on December 1. Khrushchev reacted as anticipated, although contributing rather earthy artistic critiques:"What's the good of a picture like this? To cover urinals with?;" "This is an art for donkeys;" "But your paintings just give a person constipation, if you'll excuse the expression;" and "We are going to take these blotches with us into communism, are we?"[20] A crackdown on the arts was initiated, and it extended beyond modern painting.

The Catholic Church, which had accepted the Renaissance, retrenched during the Council of Trent (1545-63) and ushered in a Counter-Reformation which deemed Protestantism heretical and reorganized the Vatican around a strengthened papacy. Leonid Brezhnev, who succeeded Khrushchev in 1964 and served until his death in November 1982, similarly rejected Czechoslovakia's "socialism with a human face" and intervened militarily in 1968 on the basis of a newly contrived "Brezhnev doctrine" founded on Soviet ideological and military hegemony. Like the Church, which expanded geographically during the Counter-Reformation due to Spanish and Portuguese colonialism, Soviet communist religiosity was spread in the Brezhnev era to Afghanistan, South Vietnam, Laos, Cambodia, Angola, Mozambique, Ethiopia, South Yemen and Nicaragua.

Domestically, Brezhnev buttressed his role as first secretary - this was signified in 1966 when he assumed the discarded Stalinist title of "general secretary" and changed the name of the party's Presidium to the former term "Politburo." Brezhnev restored so much stability to the Soviet system that it became a gerontocracy protective of its perquisites and status. The nomenklatura asserted its dominance and, as viewed by British political scientist Richard Sakwa, "the vision of the Soviet social system increasingly became one of a mechanism to be maintained rather than of a society to be transformed."[21] Brezhnev's personal primacy and emphasis on order became so accentuated that he continued to rule a superpower despite increasing physical infirmity which impaired his abilities to negotiate effectively or speak publicly. It is instructive to note that Khrushchev was overthrown temporarily in 1957, and permanently in 1964; Brezhnev's power survived for over eighteen years and terminated only with his death.

In 1559, Pope Paul IV put all writings of Erasmus on the Index. This symbolized the triumph of the Counter-Reformation over ideas bred during the Renaissance. So too did Brezhnev turn Khrushchev into an un-person and reduce freedom of expression in areas other than science. Central control was reinstituted, in part to combat the weakening of communist faith exemplified by the growing demand for emigration. In 1966, the writers Andrei Sinyavsky and Yuli Daniel were sentenced to terms of seven and five years respectively for alleged anti-Soviet acts in having their works smuggled abroad for publication. Two years later, Aleksandr Ginzburg received five years for having compiled documents on their trial.

Brezhnev's Counter-Reformation represented a step back toward Stalinism, and Stalin himself was partially rehabilitated beginning in 1965.[22] The "vozhd's" ninetieth birthday was celebrated in 1969, and a marble bust was set atop his grave the following year. Vyacheslav Molotov, who served as Stalin's prime minister and foreign minister but was removed from the Presidium and the party in disgrace after the 1957 failure to oust Khrushchev, was included in the honor guard at the December 1969 funeral of former president and 1957 co-conspirator Klimenty Voroshilov; in 1984, during Konstantin Chernenko's rule, Molotov was readmitted to the communist party. Stalinism regained respectability, and Brezhnev became the focus of extensive attention. His role in the border guards received lavish coverage, and there was even an effort to move his birthday to January 1 so it could be celebrated along with New Year's Day. It was claimed that thirteen days had to be added to his December 19 date of birth to bring it into conformity with the Gregorian calendar as Brezhnev had been born under the Julian calendar in 1906. However, it was discovererd that the thirteen days had already been calculated into the designation of December 19 so the attempt to identify Brezhnev with each new year was abandoned.[23]

The Brezhnev Counter-Reformation negated many of Khrushchev's innovations such as encouraging the turnover of party personnel and excluding the KGB director from the ruling Presidium or Politburo. Order gained predominance over vision as the assertion of central ideological and political control contributed to the regime's longevity at the expense of declining faith in communism's religious goals. Eschatology fell by the wayside as the Soviet church's guiding role became the target of increasing skepticism. A new age of reason was required to overcome societal stagnation and doctrinal atrophy, and it was soon set in motion by Mikhail Gorbachev as he led his countrymen toward the Soviet Enlightenment.

Notes

1. Roland Bainton, *The Reformation of the Sixteenth Century* (Boston: Beacon Press, 1952), p. 17.
2. See Isaac Deutscher, *Ironies of History: Essays on Contemporary Communism* (London: Oxford University Press, 1966), p. 42n.
3. Robert C. Tucker, "The Metamorphosis of the Stalin Myth," *World Politics*, vol. VII, no. 1 (October, 1954):39-41.
4. Nina Tumarkin, *Lenin Lives!: The Lenin Cult in Soviet Russia* (Cambridge: Harvard University Press, 1983), p. 259.
5. Telegram from U.S. embassy in Moscow to Department of State, July 4, 1954.
6. *Moskovskaya Pravda*, September 18, 1987 (FBIS-SOV-87-186, September 25, 1987, p. 48) and Tumarkin, p. 259.
7. See Stephen Cohen, *Rethinking the Soviet Experience* (New York: Oxford University Press, 1985), p. 102 and Gaston Fessard, "Is Marx's Thought Relevant to the Christian?: A Catholic View," in Nicholas Lobkowicz, ed., *Marx and the Western World* (Notre Dame: University of Notre Dame Press, 1967), p. 364.
8. See Vladimir Tismaneanu, *The Crisis of Marxist Ideology in Eastern Europe: The Poverty of Utopia* (London: Routledge, 1988), p. 19.
9. For analyses of the impact of the "secret speech" on the world communist movement, see *The Anti-Stalin Campaign and International Communism* (New York: Columbia University Press, 1956) and Alexander Dallin, ed., *Diversity in International Communism* (New York: Columbia University Press, 1963).
10. See Zbigniew Brzezinski, *The Grand Failure* (New York: Charles Scribner's Sons, 1989), pp. 225-27.
11. Milovan Djilas, *The Unperfect Society: Beyond the New Class* (New York: Harcourt, Brace and World, 1969), p. 204.
12. S.F. Kissin, *Farewell to Revolution* (New York: St. Martin's. 1978), p. 47.
13. See Christopher Dawson, *The Dynamics of World History* (New York: New American Library, 1962), p. 276.
14. Bainton, p. 5.
15. See Keith Bridston, *Church Politics* (New York: World Publishing Company, 1969), p. 55.
16. Anton Logoreci, "Albania: The Anabaptists of European Communism," *Problems of Communism*, vol. XVI, no. 3 (May-June, 1967):24.
17. Bainton, p. 211.
18. The execution of dissident Hungarian leader Imre Nagy may be compared to those of Jan Hus and Girolamo Savonarola, which took place during the Reformation.
19. John Dunlop, "Gorbachev and Russian Orthodoxy," *Problems of Communism*, vol. 38, no. 4 (July-August, 1989):107.

20 Priscilla Johnson, *Khrushchev and the Arts* (Cambridge: M.I.T. Press, 1965), pp. 9 and 102-104.
21 Richard Sakwa, *Gorbachev and His Reforms, 1985-1990* (New York: Prentice-Hall, 1990), p. 87.
22 The mid-sixties also featured a revival of the Lenin cult, but it subsided after the April 1970 anniversary celebrations. See Christel Lane, *The Rites of Rulers* (Cambridge: Cambridge University Press, 1981), p. 218.
23 John Dornberg, *Brezhnev: The Masks of Power* (New York: Basic Books, 1974), p. 33.

Chapter XIII

THE SOVIET ENLIGHTENMENT

The Enlightenment largely bypassed Russia two hundred years ago, but its ideas were belatedly disseminated in Soviet society with the encouragement of General Secretary Mikhail Gorbachev. When Yuri Andropov succeeded Brezhnev in 1982, Gorbachev served as a major aide and often substituted for Andropov at meetings when the latter was ill. Gorbachev was selected to present the Lenin anniversary speech in April 1983, and it appeared that he was being groomed by Andropov as an alter ego devoted to reform of the Soviet system. Andropov stressed authoritarian methods, and did not introduce the Enlightenment into Soviet society; nevertheless, he sought economic restructuring to achieve greater efficiency - a process that could be promoted by extending autonomy to economic units and reducing their subordination to central administrators. Andropov advocated fewer ideological controls and, while certainly not prepared to relinquish any communist party dominance over society, he did make a significant gesture to the Orthodox Church in 1983 by returning the Danilov Monastery for use as headquarters of the Moscow Patriarchate.

Andropov died rather prematurely in February 1984 and was followed by Konstantin Chernenko, who presided over a brief neo-Brezhnevite interregnum until his own demise in March 1985. Gorbachev then assumed the post of General Secretary and returned to the reformist practices of his mentor, Andropov. However, Gorbachev's vision of change diverged significantly from that of Andropov as it emphasized democratization and pluralism rather than authoritarianism and communist party monism.[1] As Gorbachev's reformist campaign grew bolder, he reconciled the communist party with the Enlightenment through his embrace of dissident physicist Andrei Sakharov. In December 1986 Sakharov was invited to return to Moscow from exile in Gorky, and he then played a prominent role in Soviet political and intellectual life until his death in December 1989.

Rational Humanism

The Enlightenment presented history as progress achieved through human, rather than divine, action. Faith was no longer important as man developed the freedom of ideas, economic liberty, and the rule of law through the rational application of knowledge. Reason replaced piety as man's discoveries superseded God's revelations, and religious miracles came to be viewed with skepticism.[2] Secular scholars gained ascendancy over the clergy in influencing intellectual life, and many of the most promising students were attracted to the sciences rather than theology. The Enlightenment reduced religion to a personal matter and conflicted with Christian values through its stress on the goodness of man; his negative attributes were deemed to be caused by societal conditions.[3] As expressed by historian Peter Gay: "In the older, tribal view, the blasphemer, the heretic, the unbeliever, the outsider of any description endangered the whole and had to be purged from a society he tainted by his very presence. The philosophes saw the offender not as a scourge or an enemy but as a victim, usually of society itself."[4]

Under Gorbachev there was an endorsement, to a considerable degree, of the constitutional proceduralism associated with liberal democracy; legalistic reforms took hold as they did during the Enlightenment. So too did Gorbachev harken back to pre-communist Russian values just as the Enlightenment, in reaction to Christianity, reverted to the teachings of ancient Rome. There was also Gorbachev's de-demonization of capitalist systems, similar to the fostering during the Enlightenment of a belief that individual acts of evil were divorced from any Christian concept of an all-embracing demonic force. In fact, "perestroika" sought to learn from capitalism rather than transcend it. It was reminiscent of European liberalism of the early nineteenth century, although it placed less emphasis on the market mechanism.[5]

Especially pertinent was the Soviet regime's treatment of Sakharov, a man steeped in Enlightenment concepts. Gorbachev's official reconciliation with this prominent intellectual was somewhat akin to the

Vatican's removing of Galileo's works from the Index of Prohibited Books in 1835, although Sakharov later became a political thorn in Gorbachev's side through his roles as a democratizing legislator and as honorary president of the reformist, anti-Stalinist organization Memorial. When Sakharov died in December 1989, five Politburo members, including the conservative Yegor Ligachev, failed to sign his obituary in *Pravda* but he was the subject of a tribute by a *New Times* staff writer who praised his scientific, objective and experimental method of inquiry, which was not dependent on pre-conceived ideological notions. A musical director suggested in a letter to the same publication that, to commemorate Sakharov's passing, a monument should be built to the "Citizen" as Sakharov embodied such an ideal.[6] The concept of public citizenship had been emphasized during Western Europe's Enlightenment.

The Soviet Enlightenment accentuated humanism and individualism. Anatoly Dobrynin, who headed the Soviet delegation to the April 1988 Prague conference of ninety-three communist and pro-communist parties, asserted that human interests have priority over class interests; Gorbachev also substituted humanism for proletarianism and the class struggle. The individual had come to supersede the collective, a step exemplified by changing practices in the use of psychiatry to enforce political conformity.[7] In 1988, psychiatric facilities for political dissidents were pointedly transferred from the control of the Ministry of the Interior to that of the Ministry of Health.

The communist party's platform distributed in February 1990 declared that personal liberty is man's most important value, man is at the center of social development and that spiritual fulfillment is deemed by the party to be a major goal.[8] As explained by *Pravda*, such an interpretation was consistent with Leninism as man should not be considered a means of progress; he should be its end in the form of humanism, creativity and democratic values.[9] In December 1990, an interdisciplinary conference in Moscow on humanism established an Institute of Man. In February 1991, the director of California's Esalen Institute was in Moscow to develop joint projects with Soviet institutes; according to *Pravda*, humanistic themes were discussed which transcended political and ideological differences. In April, another international humanist conference was held in Moscow.[10] The high point of the humanist campaign then came on September 5 when the Congress of People's Deputies ratified a "Declaration on the Rights and Liberties of Man." It referred to individual freedom as the "supreme value in our society" and affirmed that party or state interests could never supersede those of the individual.[11]

Despite his use of a Marxist framework of analysis, Gorbachev paralleled the Enlightenment deists in attributing progress to human action. He called for a humane and democratic socialism, an approach consistent with the early Marx rather than the later, more deterministic, Marx. Gorbachev appeared to have lost faith in achieving pure communism, so current human action was therefore enhanced in significance.[12] Rationalist humanism was the keynote. It had challenged Catholicism in eighteenth century France; under Gorbachev, it came to undermine many tenets of the communist church's orthodoxy.[13]

Withering Away

Ideology, which had often been manipulated by Soviet leaders in order to retain power, rapidly disintegrated. Gorbachev cited the erosion of ideological and moral values and blamed this decline on the stagnation of party leadership. He also criticized the media for sloganeering through which it attempted to portray success even when societal problems were evident.[14] Other factors contributing to ideological erosion were extensive economic failures, a rising demand to emigrate and the reevaluation of Stalin's crimes. Gorbachev unintentionally provided the impetus to domestic de-ideologization through his foreign policy of realpolitik, which led to diplomatic exchanges with previously shunned states such as South Africa and South Korea. Long-cherished values came to be viewed askance. One Soviet journalist referred to a "crisis of faithlessness" and growing "nihilism" and Gorbachev himself maintained that Marxism-Leninism had been distorted and had become "something of a collection of canonical texts." [15] In essence, Gorbachev wanted to rejuvenate communism; his critics believed that Gorbachev's tampering with ideological principles was the cause of Marxism-Leninism's decline.

Communist messianism lost its fervor; the workers hoped to become less proletarian and more bourgeois as a de-ideologized "post-communism" started to take hold.[16] Secularization and pragmatism replaced the previous teleological perspective since the new "post-totalitarian mind" rejects absolute truth.[17] Even *Pravda* declared that Marxism must accommodate itself to change, and the State Committee on Public Education discontinued required secondary school exams on Marxism-Leninism in the spring of 1990.[18] When secularism confronts faith, whether in communism or Catholicism of the Enlightenment, the latter is likely to suffer some disintegration.[19]

The communist party gradually substituted "ethical socialism" for its original goal of communism. The rector of the Higher Party School in Moscow, Vyacheslav Shostakovsky, recommended that communism should be dropped as the party's goal. A 1990 survey of candidates for the Russian republic's legislature indicated that only 27 percent believed that communism would ever be achieved; in fact, just 37 percent of the communist party candidates believed so![20] It is therefore not surprising that a crisis of faith was deeply affecting the party, with more people leaving it than joining (4.2 million members resigned in 1990 and the first half of 1991). Notable among the defectors were Boris Yeltsin, president of the Russian republic; Gavriil Popov, chairman of the Moscow city soviet; Anatoly Sobchak, chairman of the Leningrad (now St. Petersburg) city soviet; and Eduard Shevardnadze, who had served as Gorbachev's foreign minister. Of course, these party stalwarts were probably motivated by political expediency as well as by their reflections on Marxist-Leninist faith.

The decline of ideology reduced the party's credentials as a legitimizing force and, conversely, the weakening of the party virtually assured that communism would never be achieved. Increasing democratization and respect for the rule of law were undermining the party's status as a vanguard within Soviet society, and pluralism was replacing unity within the party itself.[21] The Enlightenment oriented Interregional Group of Deputies, formed in July 1989, included many party members and the party had become divided into factions by the creations in January-February 1990 of a liberal group, the Democratic Platform, and a conservative group, Soiuz (Union). Public confidence in the party clearly ebbed. A February 1990 poll conducted by the All-Union Center for the Study of Public Opinion, with a sample of 2500 respondents nationwide, found that 35 percent totally mistrusted the communist party, a notable increase from the 23 percent revealed in a survey the previous year. A whopping 90 percent asserted that the party had arrested the country's development, and 51 percent said that the party's aims were unachievable or no longer relevant.[22]

Gorbachev led the reforms from above, and referred to "perestroika" as a "governed process."[23] However, increasing destabilization led him to initiate a policy of retrenchment in late 1990 and serious consideration was given to the reimposition of some ideological controls.[24] The communist party still included rabid Marxist-Leninists, as was made clear by the publication of and reaction to the chemist Nina Andreyeva's scathing neo-Stalinist letter to the editor of *Sovetskaya Rossiya* on March

13, 1988. She was also instrumental in the May 1989 founding of a movement called Unity, for Leninism and Communist Ideals, aimed at purifying the party's ideological stance. There were also the ideologically faithful Marxist-Leninists appointed to top posts by Gorbachev in an effort to stem the forces of liberalization and secure his leadership role within the communist party. They included the KGB director Vladimir Kriuchkov and Interior Minister Boris Pugo, major figures in the failed August 1991 anti-Gorbachev insurrection.[25]

When Gorbachev succeeded in reasserting authority, his victory was pyrrhic as his personal political base was shaky and the communist party was under suspension pending an investigation into its role in the attempted overthrow. The party lost almost all of its power and property, and was legally banned in several republics; Gorbachev had no choice but to resign as General Secretary. In this disarray, non-communists and former communists gained the ascendancy within the constituent republics as central authority waned and the Soviet Union itself gave way to a Commonwealth of Independent States that did not include four of the fifteen Soviet republics.[26] Gorbachev's presidency ended with the demise of his country, and the communist party lay in fragmented ruins with various claimants still attempting to carry the Marxist-Leninist banner.[27]

The New Historicity

The Enlightenment led to the questioning of Biblical assertions, and later Christian claims of miracles, as science and archeology were applied to scholarship in order to determine religious veracity. The Soviet Enlightenment featured a similar examination of cherished beliefs as a new historicity evolved. The demystification of Stalin began during the Khrushchev period, but its scope was extended and new revelations are were made. Evidence indicating that Stalin's wife may have committed suicide in November 1932 was leaked from official archives. Particularly instructive was the case of Pavlik Morozov, a thirteen year old who denounced his father in 1932 for using false documents in his dealings with rich peasants (kulaks). He was murdered by kulaks in retaliation and was turned into a national hero by Stalin. Streets, camps and schools were named after him, and monuments were erected in his memory. He was then desanctified during the Gorbachev period as it was argued that he acted out of dubious morality. Similarly, the Stalinist hero Aleksei

Stakhanov was disparaged by accusations that his feat of overfulfilling coal mining quotas was staged.[28] Interestingly, Morozov came to be viewed negatively because he had told the truth, but Stakhanov because he had lied.

Nikolai Bukharin, a rival of Stalin's who was executed in 1938, was legally rehabilitated in February 1988 and posthumously readmitted to the communist party in July 1988. In January 1990, *Pravda* reprinted his tribute upon Lenin's death which originally appeared in January 1924. Bukharin asserted that Lenin did not use power to control people, but gained their support due to their love for him. Vladimir Ilyich was portrayed as comradely and as possessing a simplicity which enabled him to communicate with the masses. He had a great ability to listen to workers, peasants and soldiers.[29] Of course, the reprinting of this article was not fortuitous and was related to Gorbachev's effort to borrow some of Bukharin's economic plans. Bukharin was therefore depicted as close to Lenin, and the qualities associated with Lenin in Bukharin's account were intended to remind the reader of Gorbachev.

The move to rehabilitate the victims of Stalinism extended to the previous arch-enemy of the Soviet system, Leon Trotsky. Although not legally cleared and his views not officially endorsed, Trotsky was no longer an un-person as he was mentioned in the media, appeared as a character in historical plays, and his writings were occasionally reprinted in major periodicals. He ceased to be the Anti-Christ deemed to be responsible for many of the regime's failures, just as the Catholic Church eventually absolved the Jews for the death of Jesus.

The new historicity elevated the overthrown Khrushchev, the only General Secretary not buried at the Kremlin wall, as his role was reinterpreted as that of a reformer whose efforts were thwarted by Brezhnev. Soviet problems were laid at the door of the late Leonid Ilyich, an effort that probably had an impact on public attitudes. As revealed by a January 1989 poll conducted by the Institute of Sociology of the Academy of Sciences, Khrushchev was assessed positively by 51 percent of the respondents and negatively by 12 percent; for Brezhnev, the figures were 7 and 64 percent respectively.[30] In 1988, the Supreme Soviet ordered that the names of Brezhnev and Chernenko (his chief supporter and later the General Secretary) be removed from factories, towns and former homes and that their works be taken off library shelves.[31] Schools named after Brezhnev, and a district in Moscow, were also renamed and plaques honoring Brezhnev and Chernenko were displaced in Moscow. Andropov, who assisted Gorbachev's rise and who advocated reformism, was not treated in the same unceremonial fashion, although a town named after him did revert to its previous designation as Rybinsk. Historical revisionism created such havoc in Soviet academic circles that, in the spring of 1988, all high school final exams in history were cancelled as the existing texts were not attuned to the new historicity.

Gorbachev, in a manner reminiscent of Khrushchev but at odds with the behavior of Brezhnev, Andropov and Chernenko, stressed public accessibility and was willing to give interviews that dealt with his private life. He undeified the image of the General Secretary, but familiarization tends to undercut authority and remove elements of mystery from systems with a religious basis.[32] A revealing insight has been provided by a Siberian coal miner named Anatoly Chekryzhov who praised Stalin for evoking faith in change, even though many people were victimized; he recognized that Gorbachev was not responsible for many victims, but condemned him nevertheless for depriving the country of this faith.[33]

Vladimir Ilyich Revisited

The communist messianic vision of a classless society was largely discarded during Gorbachev's rule and doctrines regarding socialist property and imperialism rapidly eroded. The notion of ultimate truth was under siege so it was certainly not surprising that Lenin, the savior of the revolution, was being reevaluated and found to be less than perfect. This desacralization of the most holy icon of the Soviet communist religion was illustrative of communism's deterioration as a faith system, a process which may eventually reach its climax with the removal of Lenin's remains from the mausoleum in Red Square.

Lenin was turned into an historical figure and he lost his image as a religious object of reverence. It was acknowledged by party leaders that he made mistakes, and conflicting evaluations of his role appeared in the Soviet media. In an article commemorating Lenin's 120th anniversary, an historian called for pluralistic interpretations and asserted that the Institute of Marxism-Leninism should not have a monopoly on the portrayal of Vladimir Ilyich. A columnist for the weekly *New Times* proclaimed that he should not be deified or used as a symbol of the Soviet state, and she went so far as to label stories about Lenin in school books "cheap" and certifiable as "pornography."[34]

Gorbachev claimed that his inspiration came from Lenin and that Leninism provided the basis for his "new thinking." On the other hand, he repudiated aspects of Leninism on the ground of growing historical irrelevance to changing circumstances. According to Gorbachev, Lenin had to be reinterpreted and his conclusions were not to be canonized. Marxism was not a dogma for Lenin, so Leninism should not be held up as a dogma either. In the same vein, *Pravda* stated that Lenin "always gave preference to people's common sense over the chimerical constructions of ideology's teachers."[35] Questions were raised about Lenin's responsibility for Stalinism, his humanism and his roles in the killing of Tsar Nikolai II, forced labor and the initiation of terror. His patriotism and knowledge of the country were also a subject of discussion since he lived abroad for many years. *Pravda* featured an analysis by historian Roy Medvedev of the strongly anti-Leninist views of Aleksandr Solzhenitsyn; even the communist party's own journal *Kommunist* carried negative appraisals of Lenin in the spring of 1990.[36]

The new treatment of Lenin produced some curious twists. An article in a Leningrad journal reinvestigated old claims that Lenin was in part of Jewish descent and claimed that his maternal grandfather, Aleksandr Dimitrovich Blank, was actually a Jew originally named Israel. Along with his brother Abel, he converted to Orthodoxy in 1820 in order to gain access to medical studies at the university, a curriculum closed to Jews. According to this account, a Count Apraksin served as his godfather for the Christian baptism and Blank went on to become a renowned specialist in therapeutic baths.[37] In the climate of the times, it is difficult to determine whether this examination of the background of Lenin's grandfather was just a manifestation of the new openness affecting research on Lenin as an historical personage or whether it was actually aimed at undermining his image by appealing to anti-Semitic opponents of communist rule. In any case, this new assessment of Lenin's ancestry appears to have been historically valid.

Another interesting occurrence, revealing the changing fortunes of Vladimir Ilyich, was the revision of *Pravda's* masthead initiated in January 1990. Prior to that time, *Pravda* included the depiction of three medallions. One commemorated the October Revolution and two were Orders of Lenin; all portrayed the hammer and sickle. There were also two busts of Lenin and the words "Communist Party of the Soviet Union." This complex masthead was then replaced by a simple bust of Lenin, surely representing a demotion for Vladimir Ilyich and for the status of the party. In addition, Lenin was now looking toward the reader's right rather than the left as before. Could this have been ideologically significant as Soviet ideology was moving away from communist doctrines in the direction of democratic socialism? Then, after the August 1991 insurrection, *Pravda* ceased to be the voice of the communist party's Central Committee and went independent. In its first new edition, published on September 2, the format changed again as the party was no longer mentioned and there was no image of Lenin. It was indicated, however, that *Pravda* had been founded by him.

As the Soviet media reduced Lenin to a mere mortal, many voices were raised against this perceived desecration. To mark the 1990 anniversary of Lenin's birth and the 1991 anniversary of his death, *Pravda* carried tributes from Natalya Morozova criticizing those who disparaged Lenin.[38] The director of the Lenin Museum in Moscow, Olga Krivosheina, lambasted Soviet citizens who blamed Lenin for the system's faults, charging that it is similar to blaming Christ for sins committed in the name of Christianity.[39] The secretary of the party committee at a factory in Ulyanovsk, a city named after Lenin, called for the defense of Lenin from his detractors while a workers' collective in Moscow donated money for repairs at the Lenin Museum.[40] After the events of August 1991, the Lenin Museum was closed and the building turned over to the city of Moscow. Items associated with Vladimir Ilyich were sent to the Museum of the Russian Revolution.[41]

Although Gorbachev contributed to Lenin's desanctification, he continued to claim adherence to Leninism and appeared to be using Lenin's image as part of his campaign to restore party authority. In April 1990, the General Secretary gave the major address to commemorate the 120th anniversary of Lenin's birth. In January 1991, he participated in ceremonies at the mausoleum to mark Lenin's death (there were also similar programs in Ulyanovsk, where he was born, and in Gorky, where he died). In April 1991, Gorbachev again marked Lenin's birthday at a mausoleum ceremony.[42] After surviving the August 1991 effort to remove him, Gorbachev was sadly out of touch with rapidly changing political attitudes and his popularity went into steep decline. He referred to the continuing relevance of Leninism, but few gave credence to his nostalgic remarks.

Necropolitics

During the latter part of the Gorbachev era, Lenin was being de-iconized; in the words of a consultant to the Institute of Marxism-Leninism, he should not be presented as a "Bolshevik Christ."[43] His mortality was constantly stressed through references to his illnesses and funeral, and photos of Lenin taken in the summer of 1923 showed him as a frail, sick man confined to a wheelchair; several newspaper articles specifically discussed his maladies in the spring of 1922.[44] The Brain Institute in Moscow disclosed that slides of Vladimir Ilyich's brain were on 30,000 of its slides.[45]

Lenin's funeral was recalled in the republication of tributes by Bukharin and Bonch-Bruevich, and a participating doctor described how there is a yearly meeting of ten academicians with the directors of the Lenin mausoleum to evaluate the state of his embalming. The mausoleum is temporarily closed to the public as Lenin's body is taken out of the sarcophagus, studied and photographed. Furthermore, his remarks somewhat undercut the Lenin mystique as he told his readers that the mausoleum staff also embalmed Stalin, Choibalsan (in Mongolia), Gottwald (in East Germany), Dimitrov (in Bulgaria) and Ho Chi Minh (in Vietnam).[46] A slightly differing account was presented by the molecular biologist in charge of embalming. He discussed the embalming compound and explained how Lenin's body is checked every Monday and Friday and fluid is added to his hands and head. Lenin is bathed for a month every one and a half years, and a complete examination of the corpse takes place every four or five years.[47]

The campaign to reevaluate Lenin had a pronounced effect on the renaming of places honoring the memory of Vladimir Ilyich. Leninabad in the Tadzhik republic reverted to its original name of Khudzhand, Leninakan in Armenia was switched to Gyumri, the Lenin subway station in Moscow became Tsaritsyno, Lenin Square in Baku, Azerbaijan was changed to Freedom Square, and Lenin Avenue in Vilnius, Lithuania was renamed Gediminas Avenue. However, the real key to Leninism lay in the former Leningrad, previously known as St. Petersburg and Petrograd. During the spring of 1991, controversy raged over a planned, non-binding referendum in which the voters were to indicate their preference for retaining Leningrad as their city's name or changing it back to St. Petersburg. An appeal from Gorbachev in favor of continued honoring of Lenin was printed in *Pravda* and read over Soviet television. *Pravda* even went so far as to print a statement from exiled anti-communist Aleksandr Solzhenitsyn in which he rejected the designation "St. Petersburg" due to its Germanic origin. He favored a good Russian name such as "Petrograd" or, if the term "saint" were to be included, he advocated the Russified form "Svyato-Petrograd."[48] On June 12, 1991, Leningraders by a margin of 55 percent to 45 percent opted for "St.

Petersburg." Official approval of a name change required action by the Russian parliament, a step taken on September 6 by the Presidium of the Supreme Soviet of the Russian republic. Thus the name "St. Petersburg" was revived and the newspaper *Leningradskaya Pravda* became the *Sankt-Peterburgskiye Vedomosti* (St. Petersburg Gazette).

Lenin monuments were torn down or defaced throughout the country. During the particularly explosive summer of 1990, destruction on a large scale took place in Ukraine, Moldova, Georgia, Armenia, Latvia and Lithuania. City councils frequently authorized such acts, as in Lvov, Ukraine where an overwhelming majority of 116 to 8 voted to tear down a twenty foot monument.[49] A reaction to such destruction soon developed, leading to declarations by party officials in Lithuania and Kyrgyzstan condemning vandalization or removal of Lenin memorials.[50] On October 13, Gorbachev issued a decree forbidding the desecration of Lenin monuments, but *New Times* columnist Natalya Ivanova paid little heed as she called them a humiliation before the world which did not "befit a civilized society."[51] Some supported the tearing down of monuments, but claimed that Lenin was not the target. Their wrath was directed at what he had become posthumously, a symbol of the Soviet system, and they felt that his memory was cheapened by statues devoid of artistic merit. They pointed out that an edict of 1918 on the dismantling of tsarist monuments took their artistic qualities into account, and many were thus saved for posterity.[52]

An upsurge of anti-Leninism then developed after the August 1991 insurrection by communist party hardliners. Lenin statues were toppled throughout the country, including some in the capital cities of Estonia, Latvia, Moldova and Ukraine. Others were smeared with paint, as in St. Petersburg, Saratov and Nizhny Novgorod while some were peacefully relocated through the votes of city councils, as in Baku.

The most crucial aspect of the controversy over Lenin was the disposition of his body. If it was removed from the mausoleum and interred, the holiest shrine of communism would have been lost and the religious nature of the ancien regime would have largely faded into oblivion. The scientist responsible for Lenin's embalming was probably correct in asserting that those who sought to bury Lenin actually wanted to bury Leninism.[53]

Theater director Mark Zakharov, appearing on the television program Vzglad (Viewpoint) in April 1989, called for the removal of Lenin's body from the mausoleum. Yuri Karyakin, speaking at a session of the Congress of People's Deputies that June, concurred and claimed that Lenin had himself hoped to be buried next to his mother in Leningrad's Volkovskoe cemetery. A brouhaha developed over this issue as Lenin's niece joined the fray. Olga Ulyanova, a professor at Moscow State University, maintained that her uncle had never made such a request and she referred to the mausoleum as "our sacred object."[54] Natalya Ivanova, a persistent critic of Lenin, proclaimed that he should have a Christian burial next to his mother as it was idolatry and bad taste to leave an unburied "mummy" in the center of Moscow. She also recommended the closure of the research institute responsible for maintaining the embalming and suggested that Soviet leaders should not stand on the mausoleum atop Lenin to view parades.[55] Similarly, a reformist candidate in the race for the post of first secretary of the Russian communist party, Vladimir Lysenko, responded to a question at a public forum that Lenin has the right to a Christian burial; Lysenko failed to make the election runoff.[56] Amidst the clamor, *Pravda* published an article about Marx's simple grave in London, accompanied by a photo. Was this a hidden message regarding Lenin's shrine in Red Square?[57] Ironically, it appeared the day after a man had poured two cans of gasoline on the mausoleum, starting a fire. There was no damage and the perpetrator was apprehended.[58]

The body of Georgy Dimitrov, the hero of Bulgarian communism, was removed from his mausoleum in Sofia in July 1990 and cremated. Does a similar fate await Lenin? Anatoly Sobchak, chairman of Leningrad's city council, incorrectly predicted during the summer of 1990: "In a year or two, the body will be where it belongs and the news will be on the third page."[59] In September 1991, at a session of the Congress of People's Deputies, Sobchak requested that Lenin be buried next to his mother "with all fitting honors." Gorbachev successfully secured a delay on the matter, maintaining that it should be handled by the Supreme Soviet.[60] When this smaller legislative body convened in late October, it became embroiled in urgent debates about the fragmentation of the country; the disposition of Lenin's corpse was not subjected to a vote. As the Soviet Union became obsolescent, the Supreme Soviet ceased to exist and Lenin's mummy remained in the Red Square mausoleum.

Filling the Void

The Soviet Union experienced the Enlightenment in a manner that appeared to be the reverse of the West European experience. In France and other Christian states, the power of the church was eroded as a process of secularization took hold. In the Soviet Union, the dominant communist church lost its influence so secularization was actually the movement away from atheism and toward increased acceptance of theistic religion.

Gorbachev exhibited a more accommodating approach to theistic religions in 1987-88, saying that spiritual-minded believers should be treated with respect.[61] Perhaps he really believed that the free exercise of religion was a civil right, or he may have acted out of a personal hidden attraction originally nurtured by his mother. Political motivation was also conceivable as he may have been trying to align with the newly religious intelligentsia, striving to attract Western aid and investment, or attempting to divide opposition to his rule on the basis of religiosity.[62] In any case, Gorbachev gained public good will by legitimizing Christian practices and welcoming the June 1988 celebrations of the church's millenium in Russia. Gorbachev met with Patriarch Pimen (who had assumed office in June 1971 following the April 1970 death of Patriarch Aleksei) in April of that year, and the Christmas address by the Pope was broadcast for the first time on Soviet television that December.

Openness toward religion had immediate repercussions in the Baltic states. Religious programming was carried on state-owned radio stations, Latvia and Lithuania made Christmas an official holiday, and Latvia turned St. John's Day (June 24) and Lithuania All Saints Day (November 1) into legal holidays. In December 1989, the first public Christmas celebration took place in Vilnius, Lithuania where a decorated tree was placed in the city's center. Also in 1989, the right of churches to own property was enhanced and permission was granted to provide children with a religious education. By October 1, 1990, there was a freedom of religion law that included the right to disseminate religious propaganda. Between January 1, 1985 and July 1, 1990, the number of officially registered religious associations in the Soviet Union rose from 12,438 to 18,666.[63]

The resurgence of theistic religion led to the appointment of a commission in July 1989 to arrange for the Christian reburial of Tsar Nikolai II and his murdered royal family. In August, a political movement opposed to Marxism-Leninism called the Russian Christian Democratic Union was established. That September, relics associated with Bishop Mitrophan of Voronezh (who died in 1702 and was canonized in 1832) were removed from a museum and returned to the Cathedral of the Holy Virgin.[64] Also significant was a *Pravda* account by a reporter in Jerusalem who presented a highly favorable evaluation of Jesus. He wrote that Jesus operated in accordance with humanitarian and democratic principles, advocated justice and promoted non-violent social revolution.[65]

Patriarch Pimen died in May 1990 and was replaced by Aleksei II, who was received by Gorbachev on June 12. This followed a rather unusual April meeting between Gorbachev and Sun Myung Moon, leader of the rabidly anti-communist Unification Church. In March, Moon had donated $100,000 to restore the offices of the *Moscow News* in the aftermath of a fire.[66] In April 1991, Patriarch Aleksei II appeared on Soviet television for more than four hours as he conducted Easter services at the Cathedral of the Epiphany. Prime Minister Valentin Pavlov was in attendance, as was the erstwhile communist and president of the Russian republic Boris Yeltsin. The next day, Aleksei presided over services within the Kremlin walls in the Cathedral of the Assumption. On June 27, he was received by Gorbachev in the Kremlin.[67]

Patriarch Aleksei II's religious authority received increasing political sanction, a process strengthened when he spoke out against the August 1991 insurrection and anathematized its leaders.[68] He then appeared with Yeltsin at a Moscow victory celebration. The Patriarch continued to play a well-publicized role, and his January 1992 Christmas service was attended by Yeltsin. He then left on a good will visit to the United States.

Theistic religions are in the ascendancy in Russia, and some other components of the Commonwealth of Independent States, while Marxism-Leninism is in decline. The communist church had resembled Rome under siege during the nineteenth century, but it proved incapable of withstanding the forces of Enlightenment and maintaining its existence as a Vatican-style enclave with religious influence but diminished secular power. Whether communist believers will be able to reorganize as a coherent and effective spiritual movement amidst the volatile fragments of the former Soviet Union remains to be seen.

Notes

1. See Richard Sakwa, *Gorbachev and His Reforms, 1985-1990* (New York: Prentice-Hall, 1990), p. 105.
2. Allan Bloom response to Francis Fukuyama, "The End of History?," *The National Interest*, no. 16 (Summer, 1989):20; Gerald Cragg, *The Church and the Age of Reason, 1648-1789* (Grand Rapids, Michigan: William Eerdmans, 1960), p. 13 and Milan Machovec, *A Marxist Looks at Jesus* (Philadelphia: Fortress Press, 1976), p. 209. The Jesuits, who had been instrumental in spreading the faith during the Counter-Reformation, were suppressed by the Vatican in 1773 and not restored to official favor until 1814.
3. Frank Manuel, *The Enlightenment* (Englewood Cliffs: Prentice-Hall, 1965), pp. 1 and 4-5 and Czeslaw Milosz, *The Captive Mind* (New York: Vintage Books, 1951), p. 197. The transition from theology to science, and from supernaturalism to reason, may be seen in the sequential interpretations offered in the Declaration of Independence, which avers that human freedom derives from a divine source; the Declaration of the Rights of Man, which does not mention God; and *The Communist Manifesto*, which rejects God and propounds a scientific basis for man's behavior. See Lester DeKoster, *Communism and Christian Faith* (Grand Rapids, Michigan: William Eerdmans, 1956), p. 4.
4. Peter Gay, *The Enlightenment: An Interpretation* (New York: Knopf, 1969), p. 399.
5. Sakwa, pp. 57 and 373; Paul Tillich, *The Protestant Era* (Chicago: University of Chicago Press, 1948), p. xx and Fukuyama, p. 12. For an early and influential analysis of the need for economic reform and its ramifications, written in 1983, see Tatiana Zaslavskaya, "The Novosibirsk Report," *Survey*, vol. 28, no. 1 (Spring, 1984):88-111.
6. Aleksandr Pumpyansky, *New Times*, no. 2 (January 9-15, 190):43 and *ibid.*, p. 2. Sakharov and Galileo were similar in that they did not permit dominant belief systems to interfere with their scientific investigations.
7. Zbigniew Brzezinski, *The Grand Failure* (New York: Charles Scribner's Sons, 1989), pp. 190-91; Sakwa, p. 114 and Jan Feldman, "New Thinking About the 'New Man': Developments in Soviet Moral Theory," *Studies in Soviet Thought*, vol. 38, no. 2 (August, 1989):158-61.
8. Tass, February 12, 1990 (cited in *The New York Times*, February 14, 1990, p. A12).
9. *Pravda*, March 7, 1990, p. 1.
10. *Pravda*, January 7, 1991, p. 3; February 6, 1991, p. 6 and April 12, 1991, p. 5.
11. The text appears in *The New York Times*, September 7, 1991, p. 5.

12 For parallels to religious interpretations, see Yuri Furmanov, "Renewing Christ and Marx," *New Times*, no. 22 (May 29-June 4, 1990):31; Sakwa, p. 115 and Gottfried Kuenzlen, "Secular Religion and Its Futuristic-Eschatological Conceptions," *Studies in Soviet Thought*, vol. 33, no. 3 (1987):212.
13 Peter Nichols, *The Politics of the Vatican* (New York: Praeger, 1968), p. 75. Ninian Smart, a professor of religion, maintains that Protestantism redirected Christianity toward the human element, while Catholicism retained an emphasis on the divine nature of Christ. In this sense, Gorbachev may be seen as Protestantizing the church. See *Worldviews: Crosscultural Explorations of Human Beliefs* (New York: Charles Scribner's Sons, 1983), p. 123.
14 Mikhail Gorbachev, *Perestroika* (New York: Harper and Row, 1987), p. 21. See also Milovan Djilas, interview in *New Times*, no. 10 (March 6-12, 1990):16. A decline of faith may be related to extensive obedience to the communist party. Raymond Aron has written that religious experience loses authenticity when moral virtue is subordinated to obedience to a church. See *The Opium of the Intellectuals* (New York: W.W. Norton, 1957), p. 323.
15 Furmanov, p. 32 and *The New York Times*, July 26, 1991, p. 1A.
16 Dale Vree, *On Synthesizing Marxism and Christianity* (New York: John Wiley, 1976), p. 129; Aron, p. 83 and Brzezinski, p. 252.
17 Sakwa, pp. 29 and 124 and Jeffrey Goldfarb, *Beyond Glasnost* (Chicago: University of Chicago Press, 1989), p. xxi.
18 *Pravda*, April 29, 1990, p. 5.
19 See Nichols, p. 354.
20 Furmanov, p. 32; BBC interview with Vyacheslav Shostakovsky, June 19, 1990 (FBIS-SOV-90-130, July 6, 1990, p. 59) and *New Times*, no. 11 (March 13-19, 1990):2.
21 See David Satter response to Fukuyama, p. 96.
22 *Moscow News*, April 15, 1990, p. 7 (FBIS-SOV-90-077, April 20, 1990, p. 52).
23 Gorbachev, p. 56.
24 See "Z" (Martin Malia), "To the Stalin Mausoleum," *Daedalus*, vol. 119, no. 1 (Winter, 1990):338.
25 Shortly after Gorbachev resigned as General Secretary and called for the disbanding of the communist party's Central Committee, a group including Andreyeva called the Bolshevik Platform announced that it had expelled Gorbachev from the party for betraying Lenin and the revolution. See Radio Rossiia Network, September 4, 1991 (FBIS-SOV-91-172, September 5, 1991, p. 31).
26 Estonia, Latvia, Lithuania and Georgia were not members of the CIS. Azerbaijan was originally a member. It later withdrew, only to rejoin again. Georgia also reversed course and joined the CIS.

The Soviet Enlightenment   159

27 For an analysis of neo-communist parties operating after the demise of the Soviet Union, see *The New Statesman* (May 1, 1992):12-13.
28 *The New York Times*, March 21, 1988, p. 1 and Feldman, p. 147.
29 *Pravda*, January 21, 1990, p. 3 (reprinted from *Pravda*, January 24, 1924).
30 Tass, January 31, 1989 (FBIS-SOV-89--020, February 1, 1989, pp. 68-69).
31 *The New York Times*, August 17, 1988, pp. A1 and 5 and December 30, 1988, p. A6.
32 See Nichols, p. 345.
33 *The New York Times*, January 16, 1990, p. A10.
34 *Pravda*, April 3, 1990, p. 4 and Tatiana Ivanova, "Just Between Us Human Beings," *New Times*, no. 5 (February 5-11, 1991):39-40.
35 Steven Kull, "Dateline Moscow: Burying Lenin," *Foreign Policy*, no. 78 (Spring, 1990):173-75; Gorbachev, pp. 25-26; *Pravda*, April 21, 1990, pp. 1-2 and March 7, 1990, p. 1. Lenin is often reinterpreted in terms of democratic socialist values. See Brzezinski, p. 49.
36 Tatiana Ivanova, "Tin Gods," *New Times*, no. 46 (November 13-16, 1990):18; Kull, p. 177; *The New York Times*, June 8, 1988, pp. A1 and 12; *Pravda*, April 15, 1991, pp. 1 and 3 and December 29, 1989, p. 4; and *Kommunist*, no. 5 (1990).
37 The article about Lenin's Jewish background appeared in *Literator*, September 12, 1990 and is discussed by Michael Checinski in *Jerusalem Post International Edition*, January 26, 1991, p. 9.
38 *Pravda*, April 22, 1990, pp. 1-2 and January 21, 1991, pp. 1 and 3.
39 *The New York Times*, August 25, 1990, p. 2.
40 *Pravda*, February 6, 1991, p. 3 and March 4, 1991, p. 3.
41 *Pravda*, September 5, 1991, p. 2.
42 *Pravda*, April 21, 1990, pp. 1-2; January 22, 1991, p. 1 and April 23, 1991, p. 1. In late February 1991, Politburo member and party secretary A. S. Dzasokhov praised Lenin in a speech at the Lenin Museum marking (a little prematurely) the 121st anniversary of his birth. See *Pravda*, March 1, 1991, p. 3.
43 P. Rodionov, *Sovetskaya Kultura*, June 14, 1988. Cited in R.W. Davies, *Soviet History in the Gorbachev Revolution* (Bloomington: Indiana University Press, 1989), p. 123. One Soviet journalist sarcastically referred to the April 1991 Lenin anniversary celebration as the "Day of the Nativity." He maintained that the anniversary rituals were based on a "cosmogonic myth" about the creation and composition of the Soviet universe, with Lenin assigned the role of "Creator" and the October Revolution made representative of "Genesis." See Leonid Ionin, "God is One," *New Times*, no. 18 (May 7-13, 1991):39.
44 *Komsomolskaya Pravda*, January 21, 1990, p. 1 (*Current Digest of the Soviet Press*, vol. XLII, no. 6, March 14, 1990, p. 9) and *Pravda*, November 25, 1990, p.1 and November 26, 1990, pp. 1 and 3.
45 *The New York Times*, September 9, 1991, p. A8.

46 Bukharin's article from *Pravda*, January 24, 1924 and Bonch-Bruevich's brochure from January 21, 1925 are reprinted in *Pravda*, January 21, 1990, p. 3. Dr. B.V. Petrovsky's article appears in *Pravda*, November 26, 1990, pp. 1 and 3. Gorbachev's appeal appears in *Pravda*, June 8, 1991, p. 1. Soviet experts also embalmed Agostinho Neto, Angola's president, after his death in September 1979. See "Number One Object," *New Times*, no. 38 (September 24-30, 1991):30-31.
47 *The New York Times*, December 17, 1991, p. A14.
48 Solzhenitsyn's statement is in *Pravda*, May 30, 1991, p. 1.
49 *Philadelphia Inquirer*, October 24, 1990, pp. 1A and 6A.
50 *Pravda*, September 19, 1990, p. 4 and September 24, 1990, p. 1. In May 1991, a new Lenin monument was unveiled in Iangibazar in the Uzbek republic. See *Pravda*, May 6, 1991, p. 1.
51 Ivanova, "Tin Gods," p. 18.
52 *Pravda*, January 10, 1991, p. 6.
53 *Pravda*, October 27, 1989.
54 *Sovetskaya Rossiya*, June 9, 1989 (FBIS-SOV-89-116, June 16, 1989, pp. 73-74) and minutes of the Congress of People's Deputies, June 2, 1989 (FBIS-SOV- 89-142-S, p. 10).
55 Ivanova, "Tin Gods," p. 18.
56 *The New York Times*, June 23, 1990, p. 5. Aleksandr Pumpyansky, a staff writer for *New Times*, linked communist and Christian practices when he wrote: "However, it is not the purity of an idea or an individual as such that should concern us. Otherwise we may come to worship not Christ but his body, not Lenin, but his Tomb." See "Liberation From Nightmare," *New Times*, no. 1 (January 1-8, 1990):42.
57 *Pravda*, April 29, 1990, p. 5. On October 6, 1993, Russian president Yeltsin ordered that the honor guard be removed from Lenin's mausoleum. That same day, Moscow mayor Yuri Luzhkin announced that the Lenin Museum would become a city council building. See *The New York Times*, October 7, 1993, p. 8. The museum was closed on November 17.
58 *Izvestiya*, April 29, 1990, p. 8 (*Current Digest of the Soviet Press*, vol. XLII, no. 17, May 30, 1990, p. 31) and *Trud*, May 1, 1990 (FBIS-SOV-90-084, May 1, 1990, p. 68).
59 *International Herald Tribune*, August 1, 1990, p. 6.
60 Moscow Central Television, September 5, 1991 (FBIS-SOV-91-172, September 5, 1991, p. 17).
61 See Brzezinski, p. 82.
62 John Dunlop, "Gorbachev and Russian Orthodoxy," *Problems of Communism*, vol. 38, no. 4 (July-August, 1989)102-104.
63 *Argumenty i fakty*, no. 32 (August 11-17, 1990):8 (*Current Digest of the Soviet Press*, vol. XLII, no. 36, October 10, 1990, p. 31).

64 Radio Moscow in English to Britain and Ireland, July 25, 1989 (FBIS-SOV- 89-146, August 1, 1989, p. 94) and Tass in English, September 17, 1989 (FBIS-SOV-89-180, September 19, 1989, pp. 81-82). Zbigniew Brzezinski claims that former prime minister Georgy Malenkov had a Christian burial in 1987. See Brzezinski, p. 82.
65 *Pravda*, April 15, 1990, p. 6.
66 *Moscow News*, March 25, 1990, p. 2 (FBIS-SOV-90-062, March 30, 1990, p. 63).
67 *The New York Times*, April 8, 1991, p. A5 and *Pravda*, June 28, 1991, p. 1.
68 *The New York Times*, August 22, 1991, p. A10.

WHITHER COMMUNISM?

Chapter XIV

SECULARIZATION AND RELIGIOUS EVOLUTION

Marxism emerged from the European Enlightenment and its optimistic assessment of human evolution was then introduced into a tsarist Russian society that had largely been bypassed by West European secularizing concepts. As Russified Marxism took hold politically in the form of Leninism, the Soviet system remained chronologically out of sync with its West European neighbors; in a religious context, it then passed through medieval Stalinism, Reformationist Khrushchevism and Counter-Reformationist Brezhnevism on its evolutionary spiritual path . Gorbachev's endorsement of an Enlightenment religious perspective then raised the old issue of church-state relations and, in terms of West European historical development, was reminiscent of the late eighteenth and early nineteenth centuries. Now, the former Soviet Union is undergoing a process of major political and economic upheaval, with strong overtones of nationality conflict, as it seeks its way toward a better future.

Permutations

Discussing the secularization of communism may be somewhat confusing as the Soviet Union had clearly been secular since 1917. Surely Marxism was a philosophy of secularization, but interpreting it as a religion means that it is subject to its own process of secularization. In essence, theistic religion gave way to Marxism; then Marxism was the religion that was being eroded.[1] In the Soviet Union, secularization could therefore be interpreted as a move away from communist party control over other sectors of society and as increasing acceptance of other religious viewpoints. It was evident to the Soviet leadership that Christianity, Islam and Judaism would not wither away and that official atheism was under attack.[2] In the words of a Soviet citizen, "a state that is separated from the church should also be separated from atheism."[3]

Soviet secularization included the demystification of leadership, the elimination of any pretensions toward doctrinal infallibility, and the airing of formerly heretical views of men such as Trotsky and Bukharin. Also significant were the March 1990 repeal of article six of the Soviet constitution, which had granted the communist party a monopoly on power, and steps away from ideological orthodoxy through the legalization of the right to private property. The influence of Marxism-Leninism over the educational system was also declining, and theistic religions were being given more freedom to operate.

Secularization features a world vision in which physical forces play a greater role than spiritual forces, and the supernatural is superseded by rationalism and empiricism. Divine providence, or in the Marxist-Leninist case the teleological and deterministic underpinnings of dialectical materialism, is seen as less influential than human initiative and religion ceases to be the dominant frame of reference or guide to action. Ideas depart from theological (or atheistic) assumptions as dogma gives way to pragmatism and religious doctrines, such as those inherent in Marxism-Leninism, no longer provide a source of legitimacy for the political leadership. The goals of state are divorced from religious concepts and there are no longer claims of revelation made by the ruling clergy. Reverence and awe dissipate, as evidenced by the jeering of Gorbachev at public ceremonies and calls for his resignation; conversion to the cause (by joining the communist party or professing atheism) is only minimally encouraged by the party faithful.[4]

The separation of church and state turns religion into a private matter, and some church properties are put to public use. The ruling church, which in the Soviet Union was the communist party, propagates just one of many competing religions as there is a decline in ecclesiastical authority. The institutionalized church loses its hegemony as areas previously under religious control acquire autonomy, a process apparent in Soviet "glasnost". The educational power of the party clergy is reduced and scientific principles stressing immediate cause and effect replace the previous concentration on the ultimate end, communism.[5] Institutions become more differentiated and specialized, a function of the rigid social system being replaced by a more elective one offering choices, and these institutions foster change rather than tradition.[6]

Secularization leads man to focus on his present existence rather than a promised land, which in the communist context means the fading of a utopian reality represented by pure communism.[7] As an aspect of the Enlightenment, the questions raised by man are less theological and theories of politics (such as the social contract) depart from religious roots and seek grounding in the community of man.[8] As Soviet secularization operated somewhat in reverse, since the communist party represented atheism, it was not surprising that theological religions became more influential in regard to the realm of ideas. At the same time, there was growing evidence of a form of liberalism which accentuated freedom of conscience and religious tolerance. There was also an emerging legal egalitarianism, as opposed to the theoretical but fanciful egalitarianism claimed under earlier communist rule, based upon a "glasnost"-inspired concept of procedural democracy; a burgeoning rule of law, and constitutional debate, was the outcome.[9]

Robert Bellah, the noted specialist on civil religion, has outlined five stages of religious evolution: primitive, archaic, historic, early modern and modern.[10] His historic stage may be deemed applicable to early Marxism-Leninism as it includes a concern with salvation; an elite group claims a special relationship to a transcendental existence, for which pure communism may perhaps be substituted. Early modern religion then engenders the Reformation which relates salvation to good works on earth and precipitates the collapse of the church's hierarchical authority. Parallels to the Khrushchev period are thus evident. Modern religion, surely pertinent to the Gorbachev period, is based on the decline of doctrinal orthodoxy and the ostensible purity of the movement as the focus shifts to the individual and personal ethical concerns. The church no longer provides "a prefabricated set of answers," but only the environment within which man can seek out his own "ultimate solutions."[11] According to Bellah, "modern religion is beginning to understand the laws of the self's own existence and so to help man take responsibility for his own fate."[12] Such a process took place in the Soviet Union, as did the development of an increasingly amorphous religious structure with flexible membership regulations.

Christian Parallels

The Communist Party of the Soviet Union resembled the Roman Catholic Church in that both have served an historic religious mission and, simultaneously, wielded secular political power. In 1870, the Papal States were absorbed into Italy and the pope was reduced to spiritual leadership devoid of empire. The papacy became more of a religious than a political institution as the Vatican's primacy among the Christian faithful remained intact.[13] Such a transformation in more extreme form was evident in the Soviet Union, with the party losing its grip on power and its fragmented remnants barely surviving as an ideological bastion of communist religiosity.

The Catholic Church had an uneasy relationship with the Enlightenment, especially as represented by the French Revolution. In March 1791, Pope Pius VI suspended or excommunicated all priests who accepted the authority of the French government;[14] in 1798, he was forced out of Rome by Napoleonic forces and died, ironically, in French exile the following year. However, the Church's status in France improved sufficiently by 1804 to induce Pope Pius VII to attend Napoleon's coronation. Five years later, the pope was arrested by the French after he had excommunicated the 1798 invaders of Rome but he was restored to the Chair of Peter in 1814 once Napoleon was imprisoned on Elba. Gorbachev gave his support to the forces of Enlightenment; however, his appointment of orthodox Marxist-Leninists who then turned against him in the attempted August 1991 seizure of power led to questioning of both his judgment and intentions. His authority quickly eroded as evidenced by his August resignation as General Secretary and his December exit as Soviet president.

The brief rule of Yuri Andropov parallels that of Pope Leo XII (1823-29). Both men suffered from physical ailments and have become known for their morally based campaigns to reduce the privileges of the clergy and combat bureaucratic nepotism; commitment to hard work and official duty typified their tenures. Similarly, Konstantin Chernenko may be compared to Leo XII's successor Pius VIII (1829-30) as they were elderly and infirm when called upon to serve as moderate transitional leaders of their religions. Gorbachev then became another Gregory XVI (1831-46), a healthy, vigorous and courageous pontiff who faced a revolt in the Papal States and, in 1831, enacted many administrative and economic reforms under the Church's aegis. Both men's actions were influenced by external pressures emanating from other states; soon Gorbachev and

Gregory XVI became more conservative in doctrinal matters and critical of reformist tendencies.[15]

It would be presumptuous to predict the future course of the Commonwealth of Independent States and the former communist party, but some lessons from papal history may perhaps be instructive. Accepting some congruence between the dissolution of centralized Soviet control and the waning of party secular authority on the one hand, and the Church's loss of the Papal States on the other, one can see that Pope Pius IX (1846-78) attempted to buttress his religious authority via ideological conservatism. Although encouraging reformism upon assuming office, he became alarmed by the European revolutionary tide of 1848 (Italian republicans forced him into a two-year exile from Rome) and became increasingly doctrinaire thereafter.[16] In 1854, he declared that the immaculate conception of the Virgin Mary was a dogma revealed by God. After the Papal States had been constricted to Rome and a small surrounding area in 1860, he approved the release of the Syllabus of Errors in 1864 which strongly rejected Enlightenment concepts such as rationalism, fredom of the press, and the separation of church and state.

As Rome came under siege, Pius IX convened a Vatican Council in 1869-70. Just two months prior to the September 1870 entry of Victor Emmanuel II's troops into the Italian capital, papal infallibility in faith and morals was proclaimed. As described by Friedrich Gontard in his treatise on the papacy, "Pope Pius IX was forced by sheer necessity to raise the spiritual and moral status of the Papacy, at the very moment when its temporal and worldly power was shattered."[17]

The Church retained its spiritual authority, and Catholicism remained the state religion of Italy until 1984. Its secular political role has never been restored, except for Italian recognition of Church sovereignty over the miniscule Vatican City in the Lateran Concordat of 1929. In matters of ideology, Pope Leo XIII came to terms with the social consequences of the Industrial Revolution in his 1891 "Rerum Novarum" which accepted trade unions, just wages, and a state role in the protection of the working class. Pope John XXIII (1958-63) and his Second Vatican Council attuned the Vatican to the philosophical aspects of the Enlightenment.

Moscow was not unlike Rome at the time of Pius IX's elevation to the papacy, but Mikhail Gorbachev failed in his effort to reassert spiritual authority as his secular power dissipated. Communist doctrines fell into disrepute and Gorbachev only weakened his already shaky position following the unsuccessful August 1991 insurrection when he reaffirmed his commitment to Leninism, socialist ideals and the continuing guiding role of the communist party. Gorbachev is now in retirement and his return as a source of doctrinal credibility and influence is highly unlikely. The Kremlin has clearly lost its function as the communist Vatican.

The Nineteenth Century Revisited

Francis Fukuyama, in his interpretation of the "end of history," argues that Napoleon's defeat of the Prussians at Jena in 1806 led to the triumph of the idea of liberal democracy (not necessarily liberal democracy in practice). This is surely an exaggeration as Marx rejected the Hegelian idealistic perspective relied upon so heavily by Fukuyama and he didn't believe that Enlightenment values furthered by the French Revolution could reach fruition within a capitalist context.[18] Marx therefore presented his own vision of liberal democracy, one at great variance from European liberalism, and the war of ideas continued for another century and a half. In fact, the overlay of Leninism applied to Marxism made this gulf of ideas even wider.

Now, at the end of the twentieth century, Fukuyama'a analysis of the early nineteenth century is finally becoming relevant as Marxist systems are under assault and the capitalistic notions of liberal democracy are gaining broader acceptance. Gorbachev clearly discarded much of his country's Marxist-Leninist ideology in favor of the French Revolution's humanism. Two decades ago, former Yugoslav communist Milovan Djilas presciently wrote: "Communism does not lose historic battles; it loses the battle of history, in spite of the fact, or perhaps precisely because of the fact, that it believed it held a knowledge of the laws of history."[19] Richard Sakwa, in his excellent examination of Gorbachevism, argues that "late communism" closely resembled "early capitalism" and he concurs (despite reservations regarding chronology) with Fukuyama's "end of history" reasoning when he asserts: "The irony of perestroika was that while Marxist historicism was abandoned a Hegelian historicism emerged to take its place."[20] Another observer of Soviet communism maintains that Gorbachev dismantled the system rather than reformed it, providing an "exit from communism." Market forces replaced Leninism: there was no middle way.[21]

Is there truly an "end of history," and does the evolution of the Soviet system lend support to the promotion of such an interpretation? Of course the "end of history" envisioned is not Marx's pure communism, but acceptance by anti-Marxists that there is a universal historical progression has been described as "Christianity's unwitting present to Marxism."[22] Also ironical is that those Western analysts who believed that communist rule in the Soviet Union could never be reformed are now adherents of the "we won" school that recognizes the impact of the Gorbachev revolution and interprets systemic changes as part of an inevitable process.

Fukuyama maintains that Marxism-Leninism is a spent ideology and that Soviet elites accept the "end of history."[23] However, agreement with the first proposition need not lead to endorsement of the latter. Liberal democracy does not have deep roots in the Russian culture and more traditional values linked to authoritarianism and Slavophilism are already challenging liberal democratic forces. It would be naive to believe that the war of ideas has ended; in actuality, the growth of liberal democracy contributes to the airing of conflicting perspectives.[24] As voiced by a contributor to a popular Soviet news magazine, a new history is now beginning in the wake of Marxism-Leninism's demise.[25]

Daniel Bell, chief proponent of the "end of ideology" thesis, saw "an end of chiliastic hopes, to millenarianism, to apocalyptic thinking."[26] Whereas ideology contributes competing visions of the state's response to industrialization, the advent of advanced technology necessitates administrative efficiency at the expense of revolutionary principles. It could be argued that the Soviet Union has undergone this process, but an important distinction must be made which reveals dissimilitude from the "end of history" approach. The "end of ideology" argument recognizes parallel responses to the post-industrial age - there are no ideological victors. The "end of history" argument is the celebratory exultation of anti-communists who see the triumph of the idea of liberal democracy as verification of capitalism's inherent righteousness.

The liberal democratic idea did not emerge predominant in the nineteenth century as it came to be confronted by Marxism, with its emphasis on class dictatorship, and by nationalism, which eventually reached its extreme form as totalitarian fascism. Although nationalism was congruent with the French Revolution's Enlightenment liberalism, and in a sense served as a replacement for theistic religion as Western societies secularized, it developed as its own religion and sometimes came under the sway of dogmatic ideologues.[27] Nationalism was closely identified with secular religion during the French Revolution and it soon acquired overtones of salvation, faith and immortality. As assessed by historian Carlton Hayes: "Nationalism as a religion represents a reaction against historic Christianity, against the universal mission of Christ; it re-enshrines the earlier tribal mission of a chosen people."[28] In the former Soviet Union, nationalism of the Russians, Ukrainians, Armenians, Lithuanians and other peoples is rapidly replacing Marxism-Leninism as the religious focus and it is often combined, as during the Protestant Reformation, with theistic religion to constitute a potent political and spiritual amalgam. The idea of liberal democracy has not gained ascendancy; the tumultuous and intellectually fragmented nineteenth century pattern of Western Europe is repeating itself. Aleksandr Yakovlev, former Politburo member and key confidant of Gorbachev, points out that Soviet reforms have produced social antagonisms, hostility and intolerance which he classsifies as "permanent gravediggers of humaneness."[29] The Commonwealth of Independent States, like Western Europe more than a century ago and Western Europe revisited today, will probably experience major upheavals as ideas clash; there is no cause for smugness due to the choice of liberal democracy - imbued with capitalism - that has supposedly been made. Note the political resurgence of communists (albeit of a reformed variety) in Lithuania, Poland, Hungary, Bulgaria and Mongolia following a period of non-communist rule.

The battle of ideas goes on as out from beneath the reformist communist system in Russia are emerging the resurgent Slavophiles to challenge the libertarian Westernizers. They seek to revert to pre-revolutionary values as they view Leninism as a perversion of the Russian culture. Finding solace in the writings of Aleksandr Solzhenitsyn, they reject the Enlightenment perspective of the late Andrei Sakharov and detect evil and corruptive aspects of human nature which negate any striving for perfectibility. As explained by Solzhenitsyn, a new type of authoritarianism would be the "least painful path" as leaders would be responsible to God and their own consciences; the benefits to man of such a system would be at least as great as those achieved through multi-party democracy and political freedom.[30]

Although Slavophilism is ideologically at odds with communism, some affinities exist in terms of the need for order and discipline. Common concern with the "human factor" is also evident, so it is not surprising that some degree of rapprochement started to take place.[31] Gorbachev contributed to this process when he elevated the role of the Orthodox Church and appointed the Slavophile writer Valentin Rasputin to his Presidential Council. It appeared possible that Orthodoxy would move into the spiritual void left by the failing communist religion, and that the communist party could itself be metamorphosed.

Could the party's leading role have been preserved through a major shift from atheism to Christianity? Such speculation may appear somewhat fantastic, but it is grounded in the societal perspective presented by the Slavophile writer Gennady Shimanov. He typically viewed the West as materialistic and spiritually degenerate, and there were hints of anti-Semitism in his position that Judaism could bring forth an Anti-Christ. More pertinent to the matter at hand, however, was his emphasis on early Christian communism and rejection of the hierarchical class structure associated with Constantinianism. Unlike many Slavophiles, Shimanov was not pro-pastoral and anti-technological and he saw the October Revolution as part of a divine plan. Although it brought suffering, it could lead to redemption through the Christianization of the communist party as it adopted Orthodoxy as a replacement for Marxism-Leninism. The party would become the instrument of God and the state structure of the Soviet Union would remain intact, but serve refocused spiritual goals.[32]

Such a scenario was not out of the question (it was even discussed during the twenties as "National Bolshevism"), but it has now become obsolete due to the disintegration of the communist party and of the Soviet Union itself. However, Russia could evolve in such a direction as public disorder and deteriorating economic conditions produce a fusion of Slavophilism and Marxism-Leninism directed at the restoration of discipline and the resubordination of the individual to the collective interest. The political rise of Vladimir Zhirinovsky may indeed be linked to such a phenomenon.

Liberal democracy has not been solidified, and the contest of ideas continues. The quest for a new set of values will probably make religiosity an important component of the emerging, post-communist social structure as the Soviet communist religion makes way for the resurgent forces of Christianity and Islam blended, in the case of many republics, with militant nationalism. Contrary to Marx's predictions, religion will survive as part of the former Soviet Union's superstructure despite decades of communist rule - in fact, religion was instrumental throughout the Soviet period as atheistic communism strongly exhibited its traits.

Notes

1. See Owen Chadwick, *The Secularization of the European Mind in the Nineteenth Century* (Cambridge: Cambridge University Press, 1975), pp. 66-67.
2. George Kline, *Religious and Anti-Religious Thought in Russia* (Chicago: University of Chicago Press, 1968), p. 162.
3. Letter to the editor of *Ogonyok* cited by Bill Keller, "Dear Comrade Editor," *The New York Times Magazine*, September 9, 1990, p. 70.
4. Larry Shiner, "Toward a Theory of Secularization," *Journal of Religion*, Vol. 44-45 (October, 1965):284; Jacques Ellul, *The New Demons* (New York: Seabury Press, 1975), p. 23; Donald Smith, *Religion and Political Development* (Boston: Little, Brown, 1970), p. 16 and David Martin, *The Religious and the Secular* (New York: Schocken, 1969), pp. 50-54.
5. Martin, p. 48; Bryan Wilson, *Religion in Secular Society* (Baltimore: Penguin, 1966), pp. 14 and 79; and Bernard Meland, *The Secularization of Modern Cultures* (New York: Oxford University Press, 1966), pp. 69-70.
6. Gino Germani, "Secularization, Modernization, and Economic Development," in S.N. Eisenstadt, ed., *The Protestant Ethic and Modernization* (New York: Basic Books, 1968), p. 345.
7. See Ellul, pp. 25-28.
8. Alasdair MacIntyre, *Marxism and Christianity* (New York: Schocken, 1968), pp. 1-2. In the social contract, God-made law is replaced by man-made law.
9. Vadim Borisov, a church historian who decries the decline of religious authority during the Enlightenment, has an interesting perspective on secularization and the rule of law when he writes: "Rationalism, positivism and materialism, developing in opposition to religion, successively destroyed the memory of this absolute source of human rights. The unconditional equality of persons before God was replaced by the conditional equality of human individuals before the law." See "Personality and National Awareness," in Aleksandr Solzhenitsyn, ed., *From Under the Rubble* (Boston: Little, Brown, 1974), p. 200.
10. Robert Bellah, *Beyond Belief* (New York: Harper and Row, 1970), pp. 31-45. The evolution of Marxism has been likened to that of Christianity, Islam and Buddhism. See S.F. Kissin, *Farewell to Revolution* (New York: St. Martin's, 1978), pp. 65-81.
11. Bellah, pp. 43-44.
12. Bellah, p. 42.
13. See Kenneth Latourette, *The Nineteenth Century in Europe: Background and the Roman Catholic Phase*, vol. I (New York: Harper and Brothers, 1958), p. 204.
14. Friedrich Gontard, *The Chair of Peter* (New York: Holt, Rinehart and Winston, 1964), p. 483.

15 Latourette, pp. 257-58 and 265.
16 Latourette, pp. 267-71.
17 Gontard, p. 502.
18 Francis Fukuyama, "The End of History?," *The National Interest*, no. 16 (Summer, 1989):3-18; Timothy Fuller response to Fukuyama, *The National Interest*, no. 17 (Fall, 1989):93 and Richard Sakwa, *Gorbachev and His Reforms, 1985-1990* (New York: Prentice-Hall, 1990), p. 373.
19 Milovan Djilas, *The Unperfect Society: Beyond the New Class* (New York: Harcourt, Brace and World, 1969), p. 261.
20 Sakwa, pp. 377-78.
21 Martin Malia ("Z"), "To the Stalin Mausoleum," *Daedalus*, vol. 119, no. 1 (Winter, 1990):335-36.
22 Leon Wieseltier response to Fukuyama, *The National Interest*, no. 17 (Fall, 1989):15.
23 Fukuyama, p. 17.
24 Samuel Huntington response to Fukuyama, *The National Interest*, no. 17 (Fall, 1989):9 and Wieseltier, pp. 13-14.
25 Elgiz Pozdnyakov, "The End of History?," *New Times*, no. 2 (January 9-15, 1990):35.
26 Daniel Bell, *The End of Ideology* (Glencoe: Free Press, 1960), pp. 369-70.
27 See Smith, p. 116.
28 Carlton J.H. Hayes, *Essays on Nationalism* (New York: Macmillan, 1941), p. 124. For discussions of nationalism as a religion, see pp. 95-124 and Carlton J.H. Hayes, *Nationalism: A Religion* (New York: Macmillan, 1960).
29 Aleksandr Yakovlev, "New Sociality Born," *New Times*, no. 44 (October 30-November 5, 1990):5.
30 Aleksandr Solzhenitsyn, "As Breathing and Consciousness Return," in Solzhenitsyn, pp. 22-24.
31 Darrell Hammer, "Alternative Visions of the Russian Future: Religious and Nationalist Alternatives," *Studies in Comparative Communism*, vol. 20, nos. 3-4 (Autumn-Winter, 1987):275.
32 Hammer, pp. 270-71; John Dunlop, *The New Russian Nationalism* (New York: Praeger, 1985), chapter 7 and Jane Ellis, *The Russian Orthodox Church* (Bloomington: Indiana University Press, 1986), pp. 343-44.

Index

A

Adzhubei, Aleksei, 6
Afghanistan, 135
Agursky, Mikhail, 50
Albania, 132-34
Aleksei, Patriarch, 126, 134
Aleksei II, Patriarch, 155
Almond, Gabriel, 83
Altizer, Thomas, 81
Amana Community, 93
Amos, 14, 23
Anabaptism, 102, 134
Andreyeva, Nina, 145, 146, 158
Andropov, Yuri, 97, 141, 147, 148, 166
Angola, 135, 160
Anti-Christ, 3, 26, 27, 45, 47, 133, 147, 171
Antiochus Epiphanes, 24
Anti-Semitism, 4, 13, 15, 122, 149, 171
Apocalypticism, 19, 20, 24, 28, 31, 35
Aquinas, Thomas, 95, 99, 100
Aristotle, 93, 99
Armageddon, 26, 29, 31
Armenia, 151, 152, 170
Aron, Raymond, 2, 86, 120, 158
Ashkhabad, 134
Assyria, 24
Atheism, 1, 2, 6, 9, 17, 29, 33-37, 45, 48, 58, 71, 80, 83, 109, 110, 125, 126, 134, 135, 154, 164, 171
Augustine, St., 31
Aune, David, 20, 25, 31
Azerbaijan, 151

B

Babylonia, 24,25
Baku, 151, 152
Baptist church, 47, 112
Barmby, John Goodwyn, 93

Bell, Daniel, 169
Bellah, Robert, 80, 165
Bely, Andrei, 47
Berdyaev, Nicolas, 15, 33, 44, 48, 81. *See also* "God-seekers"
Berlin, Isaiah, 15, 20
Beza, Theodore, 134
Billington, James, 45
Blank, Aleksandr, 149
Bloch, Ernst, 24
Blok, Aleksandr, 47
Bloom, Allan, 40
Boff, Leonardo, 95
Bogdanov, Aleksandr, 49-51, 61, 114. *See also* "God-builders"
Bologna, 50
Bolsheviks, *see* Communist Party of the Soviet Union
Bonaparte, Napoleon, 87, 166, 168
Bonch-Bruevich, Vladimir, 47-49, 58-60, 111, 117, 151
Book of Revelation, 4, 23, 25
Borisov, Vadim, 173
Brezhnev, Leonid, 5, 100, 129, 135, 136, 141, 147, 148, 163
Brinton, Crane, 2, 17, 43, 48
Brodsky, Iosif, 71
Bruno, Giordano, 101
Brzezinski, Zbigniew, 161
Buber, Martin, 19
Buddhism, 15, 80, 98, 113, 173
Bukhara, 110
Bukharin, Nikolai, 60, 125, 147, 151, 164
Bulgakov, Sergei, 45, 48, 54. *See also* "God-seekers"
Bulgaria, 151, 153, 170
Bullitt, William, 2
Byelorussia (Belarus), 3

C

Calvinism, 17, 134
Cambodia, 135

Campanella, Tommaso, 49, 93, 115
Canada, 47
Capri, 49, 50
Cathedral of the Assumption, 155
Cathedral of the Epiphany, 155
Cathedral of the Holy Virgin, 155
Catholicism, 2, 4, 6, 9, 49, 60, 63, 67, 69, 72, 80, 83-85, 87, 93-103, 110, 124, 126, 129, 130, 132, 133, 135, 143, 144, 147, 157, 158, 166-68
Central Committee of the Communist Party of the Soviet Union, 73, 98, 131, 150, 158
Chadwick, Owen, 36
Chambers, Whittaker, 44
Chekryzhov, Anatoly, 148
Chernenko, Konstantin, 136, 141, 147, 148, 166
China, 123, 129, 132-34
Christ, *see* Jesus
Christmas, 1, 113, 154
Clement VII, Pope, 132
College of Cardinals, 94, 99
Commonwealth of Independent States, 146, 155, 158, 167, 170
Communist International (Comintern), 43, 69, 97-99, 106, 123
Communist Party of the Soviet Union, 1, 4, 7, 43-47, 49-51, 54, 57, 63, 65, 73, 81, 82, 85, 88, 91, 94, 96, 98-100,103, 109, 110, 114, 115, 119, 124, 125, 130, 131, 141, 143-46, 149, 153, 164, 166
Communist Youth League (Komsomol), 111, 113
Comte, Auguste, 54, 88
Confucianism, 80
Congress of People's Deputies, 143, 152, 153
Constantine, 48, 94, 109, 171
Constantinople, 48
Conyers, A.J., 68

Copernicus, Nicolas, 101
Council of Ministers, 131
Council of People's Commissars (Sovnarkom), 111, 114
Council of Trent, 135
Counter-Reformation, 5, 99, 129, 134-36, 157, 163
Crossman, Richard, 71
Crusades, 4, 119, 123
Cultural Revolution, 134
Curia, 99
Czechoslovakia (Czech Republic), 9, 16, 67, 135

D

Daniel, 23-25
Daniel, Yuli, 136
David, 29
Dawson, Christopher, 23
Debray, Regis, 33, 59, 81
DeKoster, Lester, 35
Determinism, 4, 17, 32, 85, 144, 164
Deutscher, Isaac, 59
Dialectical materialism, 16, 29, 35, 36, 68, 96, 164
Dictatorship of the proletariat, 4, 43
Dietzgen, Joseph, 54
Diggers, 101
Dimitrov, Georgy, 151, 153
Djilas, Milovan, 76, 128, 158, 168
Dobrynin, Anatoly, 143
"Doctors' plot", 129
Dodd, Bella, 70
Dostoyevsky, Fyodor, 44
Dukhobors, 47, 112
Duma, 51
Duranty, Walter, 65
Dzasokhov, A.S., 159

E

Easter, 1, 61, 113, 123, 155
Eastern Europe, 7
Eastman, Max, 68
Eden, Garden of, 26, 27

Egypt, 26, 28, 62
Engels, Friedrich, 83, 112
England, *see* Great Britain
"End of days", 15, 20-29
"End of history", 168, 169
"End of ideology", 169
Enlightenment, 5, 43, 67, 80, 86, 88, 93, 137, 141-55, 163, 165-70, 173
Enoch, 24, 25
Erasmus, Desiderius, 130, 136
Erikson, Erik, 90, 91, 106
Eschatology, 15-17, 19, 20, 23, 24, 33, 35, 45, 86, 103, 136
Essenes, 25
Estonia, 113, 152, 158
Ethiopia, 135
Exodus, 26, 28, 35
Ezekiel, 14, 16, 24, 25, 86

F

Fascism, 169. *See also* Nazism
Fast, Howard, 68
Feuerbach, Ludwig, 13, 34, 54
Finland, 111
Fischer, Louis, 59, 60
Florence, 123
France, 33, 68, 86-88, 120, 144, 154, 166, 168, 169
Fromm, Erich, 36, 80
Fueloep-Miller, Rene, 45, 47, 57, 81
Fukuyama, Francis, 168

G

Gagarin, Yuri, 63
Galilei, Galileo, 101, 157
Garaudy, Roger, 68
Gay, Peter, 142
Georgia, 152, 158
Germany, 13, 24, 35, 54, 97, 125, 132, 151, 168
Gide, Andre, 2, 68, 71, 72, 75
Ginzburg, Aleksandr, 136
"Glasnost", 100, 164, 165

Gnosticism, 70
"God-builders", 4, 49-51, 54, 57, 60, 61, 87, 109, 114, 115, 120. *See also* Bogdanov, Gorky, Krassin and Lunacharsky
"God-seekers", 48. *See also* Berdyaev and Bulgakov
Gontard, Friedrich, 167
Goode, Dorothy, 69
Gorbachev, Mikhail, 5, 6, 9, 73, 91, 95, 98, 100, 137, 141-55, 158, 163, 165-70
Gorky, Maksim, 46, 49-51, 58, 61, 114, 115, 122. *See also* "God-builders"
Gottwald, Klement, 151
Great Britain, 13, 67, 71, 93, 132, 135
Great Leap Forward, 134
Great Purge, 122, 123
Gregory VII, Pope, 83, 119, 123
Gregory IX, Pope, 123
Gregory XVI, Pope, 166, 167
Gutenberg, Johannes, 95

H

Hall of Columns, 58, 121, 124
Hayes, Carlton, 169
Hegel, Georg, 13, 33-35, 168
Heizer, James, 121
Herberg, Will, 26, 27
Heresy, 9, 84, 101, 102, 120, 123, 124, 164
Heschel, Abraham, 13, 14
Hinduism, 98
Ho Chi Minh, 151
Hoffer, Erich, 67, 70
Hosea, 14
Humanism, 34, 50, 51, 142-44, 168, 170
Hungary, 67, 123, 132, 134, 139, 170
Hus, Jan, 139
Hyde, Douglas, 67, 73

I

Ideology, 33, 34, 47, 48, 51, 70-73, 131, 133-35, 141, 144, 145, 149, 164, 167-69. *See also* Marxism-Leninism
Index of Prohibited Books, 100, 101, 136, 143
Industrial Revolution, 43, 167
Innocent III, Pope, 123
Innocent IV, Pope, 124
Inquisition, 4, 9, 100, 101, 119, 122-24
International Workingmen's Association, 97
Interregional Group of Deputies, 145
Isaiah, 14, 15, 24, 36
Islam, 98, 164, 171, 173
Israel, 14, 19, 24, 25, 43, 50
Italy, 49, 50, 61, 68, 71, 99, 115, 132, 166, 167
Ivanova, Natalya, 152
Ivan the Terrible, 125

J

Jacobins, 87
James, 35, 94
Jansenism, 100
Jehovah's Witnesses, 47
Jeremiah, 14
Jerusalem, 3, 121, 123
Jesuits, 99, 157
Jesus, 2-4, 6, 7, 9, 14, 23, 36, 44-48, 57-60, 63, 79, 92, 93, 95, 96, 102, 110, 113, 119, 133, 147, 150, 155, 158, 160
Job, 50, 124
John, 25, 59. *See also* Book of Revelation
John XXIII, Pope, 6, 167
John the Baptist, 4, 25, 31
John Paul II, Pope, 6
Judaism, 3, 6, 13-15, 20, 23-25, 27-29, 35, 37, 46, 50, 61, 76, 85, 86, 94, 95, 122, 123, 147, 149, 159, 164, 171

K

Kamenev, Lev, 60
Kamenka, Eugene, 96
Karyakin, Yuri, 152
Kautskyism, 100
Kazakhstan, 83
Keynes, John Maynard, 2
Khlysty, 47
Khrushchev, Nikita, 5, 6, 95, 102, 112, 129-36, 146-48, 163, 165
Kingdom of God, 3, 4, 6, 23-26, 28, 29, 45, 47, 57, 73, 81, 85, 93-95, 103, 110, 123
Kissin, S.F., 32
Koestler, Arthur, 48, 68, 75, 99
Kolakowski, Leszek, 68, 120
Krassin, Leonid, 49-51, 62, 114. *See also* "God-builders"
Kremlin, 4, 48, 57, 60, 63, 110, 114, 122, 125, 126, 131, 133, 147, 155
Kriuchkov, Vladimir, 146
Krivosheina, Olga, 150
Krupskaya, Nadezhda, 46, 60, 62, 65, 97, 121, 131
Krylenko, N.V., 125
Kuibyshev, Valerian, 122
"Kulaks", 84, 121, 146
Kyrgyzstan, 152

L

Lane, Christel, 48
Laos, 135
Laski, Harold, 95
Last Judgment, 26, 29
Lateran Concordat, 167
Lateran Council, 123, 129
Latvia, 152, 154, 158
Lazurkina, Dora, 131
League of the Militant Godless, 60, 110
Lenin, Vladimir, 2-4, 43, 46-49, 57-63, 65, 76, 81-83, 85, 94, 96, 97, 110, 111, 113, 121, 133, 140, 143, 158, 159, 163, 168

death and funeral, 62, 66, 112, 124, 147, 151
and the "God-builders", 49-51, 57, 60, 61, 114, 115, 120
mausoleum, 58, 60-63, 82, 121, 131, 150, 151, 153, 160
monuments to, 1, 152, 160
plans to move body, 2, 148, 152, 153
reevaluation of, 131, 148-53
"Lenin corners", 58, 63, 131
Lenin Institute, 58, 60
Leninabad, 151
Leninakan, 151
Leningrad (Petrograd, St. Petersburg), 1, 48, 49, 60, 62, 110, 111, 113, 114, 120, 145, 149, 151-53
Leninism, see Lenin
Leo XII, Pope, 166
Leo XIII, Pope, 83, 167
Leonhard, Wolfgang, 69
Leonov, Leonid, 121
Levellers, 101
Liberation theology, 6, 16
Ligachev, Yegor, 143
Lithuania, 151, 152, 154, 170
"Living Church", 110
London, 3, 49, 61
Lowith, Karl, 14, 36
Loyola, Ignatius, 99
Luke, 93
Lunacharsky, Anatoly, 14, 49-51, 57, 58, 60, 62, 114, 115. See also "God-builders"
Luther, Martin, 91, 101, 133
Lutheran church, 46
Luzhkin, Yuri, 160
Lvov, 110, 152
Lysenko, Trofim, 100
Lysenko, Vladimir, 153

M

Maccabee, Judah, 24
Machism, 100
Machovec, Milan, 16
Macmurray, John, 105
Malenkov, Georgy, 161
Malevich, Kazimir, 62
Mandelstam, Osip, 91
Mao Zedong, 133
Marcus, John, 87
Marx, Karl, 5, 6, 9, 13-18, 23-29, 31-38, 43, 44, 46-51, 54, 57, 59, 61, 68, 71, 72, 76, 81-83, 93, 94, 96, 97, 100, 102, 105, 109, 112, 115, 124, 133, 144, 149, 153, 163, 168, 169, 171
on alienation, 6, 27, 28, 36
comparisons with prophets, 3, 4, 14, 49, 79
and history, 14-17, 29, 46, 83
messianic views, 23-29
and religion, 17, 28, 29, 33-37, 39, 40, 81, 120
Marxism, see Marx
Marxism-Leninism, 1, 3, 70, 71, 73, 98, 100, 119, 131, 133, 144-46, 148, 154, 155, 164-66, 168-71, 173
Marxist-Christian dialogue, 5, 6
Matthew, 95, 96
Maynard, John, 46
Mazlish, Bruce, 19
McLellan, David, 40
McNeal, Robert, 66
Medvedev, Roy, 120, 149
Mensheviks, 47
Menzhinsky, Vyacheslav, 122
Messianism, 3, 17, 23-29, 33, 53, 57, 65, 106, 144, 148
Mexico, 6
Micah, 14, 24
Michurin, I.V., 100
Middle Ages, 66, 119, 124, 126
Millenialism, 23, 26, 28, 29, 45, 47, 169
Milosz, Czeslaw, 3, 69
Minsk, 63
Miranda, Jose, 6

Mitrophan, Bishop of Voronezh, 154, 155
Mohammed, 113
Moldova, 152
Molokans, 111, 112
Molotov, Vyacheslav, 83, 84, 136
Moltmann, Jurgen, 5
Mongolia, 151, 170
Monophysitism, 100
Montanism, 100
More, Thomas, 93
Morozov, Pavlik, 146, 147
Morozova, Natalya, 150
Moscow, 48, 88, 110, 111, 113, 114, 120, 126, 141, 143, 145, 147, 150, 151
Moses, 9, 61
Mozambique, 135
Murphy, Kenneth, 31, 75
Murvar, Vatro, 45, 47

N

Nagy, Imre, 139
Nazism, 86, 97
Nestorianian, 100
Netherlands, 130, 132
Neto, Agostinho, 160
New Testament, 4, 5, 46, 101, 124, 133
Nicaragua, 135
Nicholas V, Pope, 129
Niebuhr, Reinhold, 2
Nikolai II, Tsar, 149, 154
Nizhny Novgorod, 152

O

October Revolution, 44, 62, 110, 112, 115, 126, 149, 171
Old Believers, 47, 54, 93
Old Testament, 3, 4, 13-15, 23, 37, 46
Omsk, 117
Onikov, Leon, 7
Orwell, George, 97

P

Papal states, 97, 166, 167
Paris, 50, 87
Parsons, Howard, 14
Paul III, Pope, 99
Paul IV, Pope, 136
Paul VI, Pope, 6
Paul of Tarsus, 4, 5, 14
Pavlov, Ivan, 115
Pavlov, Valentin, 155
Pelagianism, 100
"Perestroika", 142, 145, 168
Peter the Great, 48
Peter, St., 3, 63, 98, 119, 166
Petrograd, *see* Leningrad
Petulla, Joseph, 15
Pimen, Patriarch, 154, 155
Pioneers, 62, 82, 123
Pius VI, Pope, 166
Pius VII, Pope, 87, 166
Pius VIII, Pope, 166
Pius IX, Pope, 6, 83, 167
Pius XI, Pope, 6
Plekhanov, Georgy, 51
Podgorny, Nikolai, 6
Poland, 3, 68, 69, 132, 134, 170
Politburo, 59, 98, 99, 135, 136, 143, 159, 170
Popov, Gavriil, 145
Portugal, 135
Prague, 9, 143
Presidium, *see* Politburo
Proletariat, 3, 4, 15, 20, 23, 24, 26, 28, 29, 33, 35, 58, 81-83, 94, 101. *See also* dictatorship of the proletariat
Proletkult, 114, 115
Prophetism, 3, 14, 19, 20, 35
Protestantism, 13, 15, 89, 93, 95, 101, 102, 112, 132, 134, 135, 158, 170
Psychoanalysis, 36, 45, 71, 72, 80
Pugo, Boris, 146
Pumpyansky, Aleksandr, 160
Puritans, 101

R

Rasputin, Valentin, 170
Rationalism, 50, 144, 173
"Red baptisms", 1, 112, 113
"Red corners", 63, 112
"Red masses", 113
"Red weddings", 1, 113
Reformation, 5, 93, 95, 102, 126, 129, 130, 132-34, 165, 170
Renaissance, 5, 126, 129, 130, 136
Robespierre, Maximilien, 87
Roman empire, 3, 25, 46, 94, 109, 142
Romania, 68
Rome, 3, 43, 48, 72, 166, 167
Rousseau, Jean-Jacques, 82, 86
Ruether,Mary, 36
Russia, 1, 44-49, 51, 53, 60, 93, 126, 141, 145, 154, 155, 169
Russian Orthodox Church, 4, 44, 46, 54, 57-62, 73, 109-14, 120 125, 126, 134, 141, 149, 170, 171
Russians, 5, 43, 45, 47, 81, 99, 170

S

St. Petersburg, *see* Leningrad
Saint-Simon, Claude Henri, 13, 88, 93
Sakharov, Andrei, 142, 143, 157, 170
Sakwa, Richard, 133, 168
Saratov, 152
Savanarola, Girolamo, 139
Scholasticism, 99, 100
Scott, James, 26
Second Coming, 26, 29, 68, 94, 96
Second International, 43
Second Isaiah, 24, 25
Second Vatican Council, 167
"Secret speech", 131
Sectarianism, 4, 47, 109, 111, 112, 114, 117
Secular religion, 1, 2, 86-88, 92, 109, 112, 114, 115
Secularization, 5, 14, 23, 40, 88, 144, 163-71

Sergei, Patriarch, 44, 110, 111, 125, 126
Seventh Day Adventists, 112
Shakhnazarov, Georgy, 91
Shakhty affair, 122
Shaw, George Bernard, 60
Shchusev, A.V., 62
Sheen, Archbishop Fulton, 2, 44, 80, 128
Shevardnadze, Eduard, 145
Shimanov, Gennady, 171
Shostakovsky, Vyacheslav, 145
Silone, Ignazio, 68, 69, 75
Sinyavsky, Andrei, 136
Skoptsy, 112
Slavophilism, 43, 44, 169-71
Smart, Ninian, 46, 68, 158
Smith, Donald, 98
Sobchak, Anatoly, 153
"Sobornost", 45
Socialist Revolutionaries, 46
Sofia, 153
Solzhenitsyn, Aleksandr, 130, 151, 170
"Son of Man", 24, 25
South Africa, 144
South Korea, 144
South Vietnam, 135
South Yemen, 135
"Sovnarkhozy", 130
Spain, 122, 123, 135
Spender, Stephen, 71
Spinoza, Baruch, 14
Stakhanov, Aleksei, 146, 147
Stalin, Iosif, 3-5, 9, 58-60, 63, 65, 66, 68, 72, 83, 84, 94-96, 99, 100, 112, 115, 119-26, 128-32, 136, 144-49, 163
Stalingrad (Tsaritsyn), 120
Sun Myung Moon, 155
Syllabus of Errors, 167
Syria, 24
Szasz, Thomas, 71

T

Tadzhikistan, 151
Talmon, Jacob, 14
Talmud, 14, 23
Tarsis. Valery, 71
Tbilisi, 120
Teleology, 16, 35, 81, 90, 103
"Thaw", 5, 130
Theodosius, 94, 109
Theology, 6, 13, 26, 29, 33, 45, 49, 80, 81, 92, 96, 157, 164, 165
Third Rome, 4, 48, 88
Tikhon, Metropolitan of Moscow, 110, 111
Tillich, Paul, 15, 89
Tismaneanu, Vladimir, 69
Tiumen, 62
Togliatti, Palmiro, 132
Tolstoy, Leo, 50
Torah, see Old Testament
Totalitarianism, 109, 130, 144, 169
Towster, Julian, 53
Tracy, Antoine Destutt de, 34
Trotsky, Leon, 4, 84, 96, 100, 122, 147, 164
True Levellers, 101
Tsarism, 47, 110, 111, 122, 125, 163
Tucker, Robert C., 25, 40
Tumarkin, Nina, 59
Turkmenistan, 134

U

Ukraine, 3, 152, 170
Ukrainian Orthodox Church, 126
Ulyanova, Olga, 153
Unification Church, 155
United States of America, 35, 44, 49, 68-70, 84, 86, 93, 96
Urban II, Pope, 123
Utopianism, 17, 31, 49, 82, 93, 115, 121
Uzbekistan, 16

V

Vakar, Nicholas, 66, 73
Vatican, see Catholicism
Vatican City, 63, 97, 167
Victor Emmanuel II, 167
Vilnius, 110, 151, 154
Voroshilov, Klimenty, 136

W

Western Europe, 3, 87, 143, 154, 163, 170
Wetter, Gustav, 35
Winstanley, Gerard, 101
World War I, 45
World War II, 119, 126
Wright, Richard, 84

X

Xavier, Francis, 99

Y

Yakovlev, Aleksandr, 9, 39, 170
Yakubovich, Mikhail, 125
Yeltsin, Boris, 145, 155, 160
Yevtushenko, Yevgeny, 5, 130, 131
Yugoslavia, 132, 134, 168

Z

Zakharov, Mark, 152
Zechariah, 24
Zhdanov, Andrei, 122
Zhirinovsky, Vladimir, 171
Zinoviev, Grigory, 58, 60
Zoroastrianism, 24

About the Author

Arthur Jay Klinghoffer is a Professor of Political Science at Rutgers University. He majored in Russian language at the University of Michigan and later received his doctorate in Public Law and Government from Columbia University and a certificate from that institution's Russian Institute. Dr. Klinghoffer was elected to Phi Beta Kappa, has been appointed a Nobel senior fellow, and has twice been the recipient of Fulbright grants. He is the author of nine books including *The Soviet Union and International Oil Politics*, *Israel and the Soviet Union*, *Soviet Perspectives on African Socialism*, and *The Angolan War: A Study in Soviet Policy in the Third World*.